AF167578

# SHARDED MEDIA

William Merrin · Andrew Hoskins

# SHARDED MEDIA

Trump's Rage Against the Mainstream

William Merrin
Media and Communication Studies
Swansea University
Swansea, UK

Andrew Hoskins🆔
School of Social and Political Science
University of Edinburgh
Edinburgh, UK

ISBN 978-3-031-84785-1          ISBN 978-3-031-84786-8   (eBook)
https://doi.org/10.1007/978-3-031-84786-8

Cover credit: © John Rawsterne/patternhead.com

This Palgrave Macmillan imprint is published by the registered company Springer Nature Switzerland AG
The registered company address is: Gewerbestrasse 11, 6330 Cham, Switzerland

If disposing of this product, please recycle the paper.

# Acknowledgements

We are indebted to Catherine Happer for her long-term collaboration with us, especially since our co-edited (2018) volume, *Trump's Media War*. We are very grateful to Sarah Oates and to Kate Wright, for their kind and expert advice on this work. It is important for us to recognise the support and guidance of these three leaders of their respective fields.

Our publisher, Palgrave, was hugely encouraging and helpful in the commissioning and the production of this work. We are particularly grateful to Felicity Plester, Richard Woolley and Linda Braus, to this end.

# CONTENTS

# About the Authors

**Dr. William Merrin** is Associate Professor of Media Studies at Swansea University, UK.

He is the author of: *Digital War* (Polity, 2018), *Media Studies 2.0* (Routledge, 2014), and *Baudrillard and the Media* (Polity, 2005), and co-editor of *Trump's Media War* (2019) and *Jean Baudrillard: Fatal Theories* (Routledge, 2009). He is Founding Co-Editor-in Chief of the *Journal of Digital War.*

**Professor Andrew Hoskins**  holds a personal chair in AI, Memory and War, at the University of Edinburgh, UK.

He is Founding Co-Editor-in-Chief of the Cambridge Journal of *Memory, Mind & Media*, Founding Editor-in-Chief of the SAGE Journal of *Memory Studies*, and Founding Co-Editor-in Chief of the Palgrave Journal of *Digital War*. He is also Founding Co-Editor of the Palgrave Macmillan *Memory Studies* Book Series.

He is the author/editor of 10 books, including *Radical War: Data, Attention & Control in the Twenty-First Century* (Hurst/OUP 2022, with Matthew Ford) and *The Remaking of Memory in the Age of the Internet and Social Media* (OUP 2024, co-edited with Qi Wang).

Hoskins leads WarShare, an ERC awarded, UKRI-funded, five-year research project (2025–30) on digital participation in war.

# CHAPTER 1

# Sharded Media

**Abstract** The smartphone's sharding of experience through personal networks favoured platforms, recommendations and peer-linked sources, splintered political awareness, experience and activity. This chapter maps the force and consequences of sharded media's smashing of mainstream news media's (MSM) hold on reality. We present the conundrum of Trump for the mainstream, sinking fast in a splintering marketplace of that which was once called news, as their most obvious, yet most perilous of saviours. He embodies the very anger-inducing, troll-baiting shards that felled them in the first place. This chapter maps the MSM's fruitless attempts to regain control over their hold over reality. By throwing moderators, fact-checkers and other verifiers, at a self-righteous pursuit of an MSM-badged truth, they failed to recognise the reality that they were trying to fix, wasn't theirs. This only served to entrench a liberal self-deception of a society of the comfortably numb. And, by the 2024 election, the Trump campaign weaponised a new reality sharding force—generative AI—collapsing truth and fiction in new black box media ecologies of impossible provenance. Ultimately, the period between Trump's victories will be seen as a historical void in the liberal mainstream's failure to grasp the splintering of realities, reflected in their final despair, resignation, and withdrawal, at the 2024 election result.

© The Author(s), under exclusive license to Springer Nature Switzerland AG 2025
W. Merrin and A. Hoskins, *SHARDED MEDIA*,
https://doi.org/10.1007/978-3-031-84786-8_1

**Keywords** Sharded media · Mainstream News Media (MSM) · Fact-checking · Donald J. Trump · Attention · Filter bubble · Generative AI · AI slop

## THE MSM RUNS FOR THE DOOR

Two days after the 2024 re-election of Donald J. Trump to the White House, the right-wing British newspaper The Telegraph was already trolling its competitor, The Guardian, bathing in the liberal/left-wing visceral trauma at the result. 'Guardian offers therapy to staff after 'devastating' Trump election win' (Burton, 2024) ran one article headline, accompanied with a grumpy photo of the Guardian's editor, Katharine Viner, and one of a smiling President Trump.

The article extended its fun to pointing out the wider liberal suffering in the US:

> some colleges have given students time off, an extension on deadlines, art therapy classes and access to a therapy duck in response to Trump's win. Students...were reportedly told this week that they could play with Lego, colouring books, and have milk and cookies in "self-care suites" following the result. (Burton, 2024)

Shock, horror, incredulity and trauma are de rigueur of the Trump era. But when shouts of *emergency!* at the firestorm before your very eyes are its greatest accelerant, when outrage is your enemy's political currency, when despair is the genesis of trolls, what can you do?

This book is the story of how the unleashing of individual public opinion and rage became the most valuable of political currency. The digital's apparent liberation of the self to endlessly express, record and share their views, opinions and experiences has both intoxicated and entrapped them. We may feel that we live in a shared world, in which we are lively through our digital acts and continuous connectivity, with others. However, these same acts serve to furrow *sharded*, algorithmically and personally-fed feeds.

A self-curated reality feeds rage, resentment, an always-on informational battle against everyone with a different opinion, against not a collective, but a new digital multitude, sharding the political landscape.

The rise of Trump is both a symptom and a catalyst of this phenomenon, embodying the public's disenchantment with liberal democracy and its embrace of a more visceral, emotionally-driven politics. Trump's resurgence signals a profound transformation in politics, yes, but also of reality itself.

It is important then to recognise media as *epistemological engines*: they create our experience, knowledge, concepts of truth and horizons of thought. In this way, what was mass-produced in the broadcast era of the twentieth century was reality itself. It was The Media, or the mainstream news media (MSM), that seduced a middle ground of America to believe that they were reality, pushing the *deplorables* to its margins, until the margins became the reality.

This reversal should have been anticipated in the long decline and 'crisis' (see Fig. 1.1) of the media. Yet the liberal shock and trauma at the result of the 2024 US election suggests a self-deception through a MSM that had for decades made a society of the comfortably numb.

To take one (fictional) warning from history, the 1976 US Oscar-winning satire *Network*[1] is a story of what happens when pent up American anger, just below its shiny surface, is suddenly given a voice. The movie shows the rageful breakdown of network news anchor Howard Beale, who turns on his employers that had for years suppressed the views and opinions of those they deemed marginal and extreme. Beale leads a popular revolt against the mainstream with his clarion call shouted out from windows onto the streets by viewers, 'I'm as mad as hell, and I'm not going to take this anymore'.

*Network* is set in an era seen by some as the 'high modernism' of American journalism (Hallin, 1994: 5) professional but insular, in which a public has grown tired and angry at a mainstream news and culture in which their voice is unheard. Beale embodies both the mainstream elite and a tipping point of a popular rebellion against its exclusive representational hold on events: 'The American people are turning us off. They've been clobbered by Vietnam, Watergate, the inflation, the depression. They've turned off, shot up... the American people want someone to articulate their rage[2]'.

In 2017, the movie found new resonance, becoming a template placed over the emergent Trump era, including leaving the screen for the stage in a new play at the National Theatre in London. Following a preview performance of the play on 8th December 2017, after the cast had left to a standing ovation, the big screen on stage began running multiple video

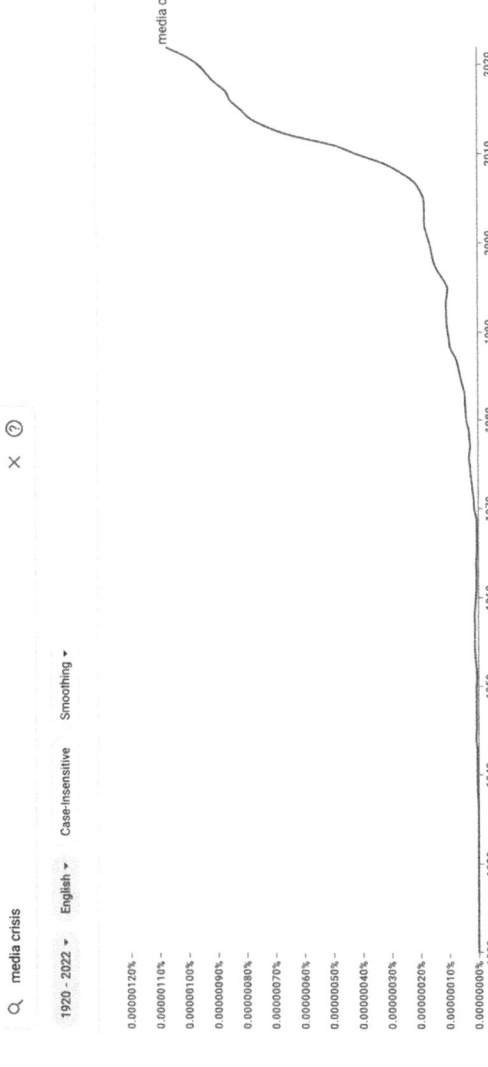

**Fig. 1.1** 'Media crisis' according to Google Books Ngram Viewer (1920–2022)[6]

excerpts of presidential inaugurations from the mid-twentieth century moving forward in time. Rather than the audience leaving the theatre, most stayed for the whole sequence as though they wanted to be part of the inevitable expression of their own rage at Trump being elected US President. There was little response through the excerpts until Obama's inauguration was cheered, but that was mild in comparison with the collective noise of boos and shouts at Trump's appearance on screen.

This kind of response to Trump fits what Dayan sees as the emergence of a 'moral public sphere'. Dayan argues: 'The main issue at hand is not: Why should I watch this? (Does it concern me?). But: Who is the villain? A Manichean grammar transforms a public sphere of 'overhearing' into a 'moral' public sphere; one which does not call for debate, but for applause or booing' (Dayan, 2013).

The era of *Network's* original production is also significant in that it marked the popularising of the term 'The Media' (Boyer, 2009: 5) as a coherent body that reflected or shaped the world out there. But somehow The Media held on to its centrifugal position in many Western societies for forty more years, despite scandal and the seething masses it disenfranchised from its mythical but dominant centre.

So, what unleashed the rage that was the mainstream's undoing? It was the global, societal and personal revolution in information technology and information, which smashed the news media order. The digital maelstrom of images, videos, messages, comments, propaganda, ideas and claims has imploded politics into informational and participative warfare (Merrin, 2018; Merrin & Hoskins, 2020, 2024). Yet this conflict is also characterised by a mix of ignorance and denial of what the mainstream has become. All the moderators, fact-checkers, BBC 'Verifiers', scholarly fields and so on, thrown at this self-righteous fight (mostly since 2007, see below), show a catastrophe of misidentification.

They couldn't see or accept that the illicit was *already* the norm. Raging at Joe Rogan is a case in point. All this time, the liberal mainstream and its believers have been trying to fix the new reality. It just wasn't *theirs*. Tech bros, Trump and trolls, have not toxified the MSM, they have replaced it. This includes Elon Musk's takeover of Twitter, the podcasting revolution and Trump's capture of the Voice of America[3] (Wright et al., 2024). It is no wonder then that all that is left for the MSM's former liberal inhabitants is melancholia, withdrawal and therapy.

The mainstream news media (MSM), the most powerful media bubble ever forged, abused its monopoly in its making. Until it broke. The

MSM's use of fact-checker ear plugs to muffle the clamour of all that it could not bear to hear is a denialism marking the advance of a post-trust[4] era. This dilemma of feeding or not feeding the monster is nicely summed up by Warzel (2024a) 'in the absence of a shared reality, fighting against an opposing information ecosystem isn't as effective as giving more people a reason to get excited about, and pay attention to, yours'. But does the exodus from X to Bluesky, for instance, mark retreat and resignation, rather than rebirth? Will the last liberal to leave the mainstream please turn the lights off.

Those who complain about the sharding of reality need to grasp how that reality was created in the first place. The MSM's principal provider that supposed middle ground, news public, audience or mass—choose your own collective label—was always a myth. After Trump's first election victory, the MSM still clung to a nostalgia of their former management of a cosy middle ground, insular and untainted by the extremes and awfulness of human action and opinion. Life on the margins was pushed safely from view. The middle ground was only ever a fantasy of journalists, news editors and owners, sustained through the MSM's monopoly as provider of a vision of the world out there.

## Deep Nostalgia

Certainly, at the time of Trump's first election, the MSM's vision of America marginalised huge swathes of the white working and middle class, negating them as a group with a legitimate mode of experience with legitimate opinions. The liberal MSM mitigated against reflecting how many people actually felt. For example, Arlie Russell Hochschild in her terrific ethnographic work found alienation among white southern right-wing supporters, who instead invested trust as part of a social terrain of institutions which included Fox News (Hochschild, 2017: 128).

One Tea Party member that Hochschild spoke with complained of turning on some of the liberal MSM (when she is abroad flipping hotel TV channels as she never watches these at home) and just finding 'opinion' rather than 'news'. The respondent continues: 'Take Christiane Amanpour. She'll be kneeling by a sick African child, or a bedraggled Indian, looking into the camera, and her voice is saying, 'Something's *wrong*. We have to *fix* it'. Or worse, *we caused* the problem. She's using that child to say, '*Do* something, America'. But the child's problems aren't our fault' (2017: 128). Hochschild argues that this response indicates how features of her interviewee's life functions to alienate her from this particular mode of liberal MSM coverage: 'The social terrain around her–industry, government, church, media–lifted focus away from such a child's needs and from her own detachment from them' (2017: 128). And it is precisely this social terrain of the right in America that the liberal MSM could neither comprehend nor reach.

Another way to view sharded media is that seeking or requiring trust of an audience to exercise power is no longer needed. One weapon of the right was to attention-hack, namely 'to increase the visibility of their ideas through the strategic use of social media, memes, and bots—as well as by targeting journalists, bloggers, and influencers to help spread content' (Marwick & Lewis, 2017). This was one of the principal conclusions of Marwick and Lewis' Data & Society report who use the term 'far-right' to characterise 'an amalgam of conspiracy theorists, techno-libertarians, white nationalists, Men's Rights advocates, trolls, anti-feminists, anti-immigration activists, and bored young people' (p.3) as the principal attention hackers.

But today, in their political influence, this amalgam of far-right groups is the mainstream. In their post-2024 election malaise, The New York Times still couldn't quite grasp being confronted with the new normal. One article, for instance, described Trump's 'new strategy', as: 'Skip most mainstream media and head straight into the manosphere, the loose caucus of podcasters, livestreamers, social media stars and other outlier media figures who have heavily monopolised online discourse lately' (Caramanica, 2024). 'The manosphere?' 'Outliers?' 'Online discourse'? There is a risk to describing influencers as some kind of transient outsiders, as though they will someday go away, to enable the return of politics as usual.

It was a deep nostalgia for its former monopolistic vision that prevented the MSM in 2016 and (more surprisingly) again in 2024, from recognising that it was their reality that was not the only one! But trying to foster a more inclusive version of *their* reality was never going to remake it. Following Trump's first election victory, for instance, there was a US mainstream journalism that believed that if only they could include others in *their* world view, if only they could comprehend the anger that brought Trump to power, then they could somehow connect with them and bring them in (and away from the margins, above). Dean Barkay, then Executive Editor of The New York Times, explains:

Here's what I think we missed and I think the entire journalism establishment of the United States largely missed: I think we didn't have a handle on the anger in America and I don't think we quite understood the appeal Donald Trump held for a lot of Americans. I think we sort of all missed this dramatic shift in the tone of the country... Discussions are very different in New Orleans etc. to what they are in New York or LA or DC. Figuring out ways to get in the middle of more of those discussions is going to be important to understanding the country... is to help our readers understand how people think who are not like them. (BBC, 2017a)

But the idea of a *shared* reality was never possible following the twentieth-century broadcast MSM's forming of a *mainstream bubble* one producing, for its inhabitants, a single enclosure of a self-reinforcing world of news, information and entertainment (Happer et al., 2019). There were no individual means for the expressing—or *producing*—of views and opinions that could pierce the bubble—besides, there was no outside to be revealed. This was not quite *The Truman Show*.

Today's digital media, by contrast, are a *bubble machine*. This is a world full of filter bubbles, of *me*-dia and personalised realities, a world of algorithmic decision-making, of multi-actor and AI[5]-generated and faked disinformation, of deluded, incessant misinformation ('filter-babbles'?), of exploded realities, and of foam worlds of personally-formed and encompassed information (Merrin & Hoskins, 2024).

But wait. Is there no hope for the return or rebuild of the former (as we now must call it) MSM? Well, kind of. The principal problem with this hope is that it is made possible by the very anger-inducing, troll-baiting media that helped fell the mainstream in the first place, a hope embodied in its greatest ever tormentor, Donald J. Trump.

It was the attention hogging horror and incredulity of Trump in the White House, his fall (of sorts), and his astonishing rebirth, that was once recognised as the singular lifeboat available to the already under water MSM, sinking fast in a shrinking and splintering marketplace of that which was once called news. The re-election of Trump simultaneously defeated and offered the MSM a lifeline, their most obvious, yet most perilous of saviours.

This paradox is not lost on the MSM's self-proclaimed slayers. For instance, Megyn Kelly, former Fox News anchor and podcaster (*The Megyn Kelly Show*) speaking a few days after the re-election of Trump, explains,

Well, look, Trump is a ratings magnet. In that way, he's revived them yet
again. His enemies, because they can't stand him, ironically, he's given
them a lifeline. I don't think CNN would have made another four years
covering Kamala Harris. She would have been incredibly boring. It would
have been running cover for her. It would not have been interesting. So,
they should be grateful Trump won…I think they are dead. They're dead,
they just might not know it yet. It's a slow death… Let me put it this way,
CNN, on election night I think had four million viewers. You know who
else had four million viewers on election night? I did. I guarantee you the
cost of my show is a teeny tiny little fraction compared to what it cost
CNN to put all of those shows and all of those people on air. It's just not
a winning business model. (BBC, 2024a)

But to use Sontag's (2003) influential line, 'does shock have term limits'?
Prior to the digital era, the surprising and the sensational always sold,
but shock and awe were once only part of any news package. The core
success of the MSM was its production and construction of a safe mythical
middle ground, where the drama that sells could also be rendered intel-
ligible and safe, ultimately reassuring of its readers and its viewers, that
everything would ultimately be ok. News amplification, dramatisation,
shock and trauma, especially on television, have always been followed by
containment, so media theorists told us (Hoskins & O'Loughlin, 2007;
Silverstone, 2002: 2). But digital sharding of the once mass audience into
a personalised click-bait attention economy has few restraints. Individuals
in personal filter bubbles source their own dopamine, they don't need it
on MSM prescription.

The long decline in trust in the MSM is hardly news, but it is digital
media, the app-enabled seemingly free access to and production of unlimited information about the world, that shattered its monopoly, and which
devalued its core product. It is no wonder then that the recognition of
media in crisis has new velocity from 2007, the year of the release of
Apple's iPhone (Fig. 1.1), empowering the individual as the supreme
producer as well as consumer of information and content.

Following the 2016 election, there was some recognition at least of
the benefits for the MSM in engaging with Trump, as we set out above,
shock, horror, incredulity and trauma are ultimately attention grabbers for
the mainstream. The more Trump goaded The New York Times as 'failing', the more it retorted with declarations of its thousands of subscribers
added for its news product since Trump first came to office. Dean Barkay,
the NYT's Executive Editor, for example, says: 'The truth is this is a great

story and people are lining up to read us' and CNN's Brian Stelter states: 'This is it! This is the moment journalists live for' (BBC, 2017a).

In the context of the digital upending of the news business and the related decline in the traditional mass news readership and audience, covering Trump became an economic necessity. And yet, with Trump's second election victory, this no longer played out as the moment liberal MSM journalists 'live for', or at least not for their audiences. Rather, the long decline and crisis have been replaced with a sudden and catastrophic fall in attention. Following the 2024 election, CNN suffered a 45 per cent drop in its prime time viewers to a total of only 394,000 (compared with the election year 2020's average of 1.8 million viewers) (Barr, 2024).

Some saw the emergence of President Trump as a direct failure of MSM journalism to effectively communicate what the liberal left saw as peril. This is a common theme in the work of the former journalist and professor Jeff Jarvis, who tweeted after the 2016 election: 'I fear that journalism is irredeemably broken, a failure. My profession failed to inform the public about the fascist they are electing[7]'. Jarvis, in a Twitter exchange the following summer with Jay Rosen, another influential liberal press critic, reflected on an impasse in how they could respond to Trump, whose survival depended upon the very media exposure and attention they were giving him.

> Rosen: 'I'm coming round to the view that we don't understand the "anger the media, win prizes" strategy. It has a logic we're not fully grasping…
> If the device works like this: "you voted for him, 'they' are trying to stop him," then critical coverage makes the Trump Machine go'.
>
> Jarvis: 'So what is an appropriate journalistic strategy in a gaslit political world? Reporting on method over message? Selective silence?'
>
> Rosen: 'Unclear. The playbook in political journalism contains no instructions for this situation. Normally that means: experiment wildly and learn'.
>
> Jarvis: 'Also requires more introspection: "How are we being used?" means admitting we are. "What to do about it?" follows… Of course, media have been used since Bernays. The added angle now is media are the enemy[8]'.

It is clear from just this Jarvis and Rosen exchange on Twitter, eight months into Trump's first presidency, that whilst the nature and the consequences of MSM decline at the time were apparent, potential solutions were not.

At least Jarvis concedes that the mass media was broken, and that some pragmatism is needed in accepting that which is beyond reach. Earlier in 2017, he reflects:

> What's a liberal journo to do? We are stuck in endless paradoxical loops. If we do our job and catch the President in a lie, we are labeled liars. When we counteract fake news with real news, everything becomes fake news. If I get angry about being attacked by angry white men I end up becoming an angry white man. Liberals tell us to be nice to conservatives to win them over but then they only mock us for being weak. Snowflakes. Cucks. Liberal tears. (Jarvis, 2017)

For all this recognition of the threat to their existence, the time between 2014 and 2024 is marked by a catastrophic inability of the MSM to arrest their decline, and the related rise of Trump. Will this be seen as journalism's lost, and last, decade? These are the final years of the MSM straightjacketed by melancholia for a time when the whole world was watching (them) (to adapt from Gitlin's (1980) famous book), their deep organisational nostalgia, unshakable. Jarvis, as a keen watcher of all this, grew increasingly angry at the refusal of the MSM, and notably what he routinely labelled on X as #BrokenTimes and #BrokenPost, to say what they see.

Following Rupar, Jarvis points to 'sanewashing', 'the practice of attempting to explain, excuse, and normalise demented, deranged, and extremist behavior' (Jarvis, 2024). This is one of a series of grievances, 'regarding political coverage coming from once-devoted liberal readers as well as experienced journalists', Jarvis lists in an excellent essay, published the week before the 2024 election (Jarvis, 2024). For decades, journalism and media studies obsessed over 'news values', namely criteria for what makes something newsworthy (Galtung & Ruge, 1965). All that is left now are *anti-news values*, taxonomies to explain why events and people shouldn't be newsworthy; is silence (Jarvis, above) or erasure, then, all that is left?

Jarvis' conclusion is nonetheless not to give up (yet). Rosen, however, has had enough. In a post on X on 8th November 2024, he writes:

> Starting Monday I won't be continuing at this site. Or as "press critic online most of the time." For a while Twitter was a way to do journalism education in public, for a public— and for free. I think I was effective at times in that role. I no longer know how that's done… Don't expect the press criticism I had been doing. I'm done with that.[9]

Two days later, the *Observer* investigative journalist Carole Cadwalladr offers her analysis:

> It began as a tear in the information space, a dawning realisation that the world as we knew it – stable, fixed by facts, balustraded by evidence – was now a rip in the fabric of reality. And the turbulence that Trump is about to unleash – alongside pain and cruelty and hardship – is possible because that's where we already live: in information chaos. (Cadwalladr, 2024a)

Cadwalladr's response to the incoming 'great Trump-Musk crackdown' was to launch a newsletter on Substack, 'because we can trust no platform & no publisher[10]'. Her first post on 10th November 2024, 'Fight the power' is headed with a photo of Elon Musk in an arms and legs outstretched kind of victory pose with his shadow falling on a huge backdrop of the Stars and Stripes (Cadwalladr, 2024b).

And yet, Substack, the very platform Cadwalladr chose to host her 'anti-broligarchy' vehicle, announced, only a month later, their partnering with The Free Press. The Free Press are not exactly known for being anti Musk, not least as 'he gets shit done[11]'. Jeff Jarvis in a post on X on 17 December makes the point: 'If *anyone* still had doubts about Substack's right-wing politics, its partnering with Free Press should erase them[12]'.

Does this all add up to our living in an age of 'information chaos' (Cadwalladr, 2024a, above)? The liberal left may well feel shock and turbulence, if not catastrophe. However, each sharded individual exists in a personally-formed and encompassed informational bubble that does afford them order and intelligibility. Diametrically opposed media ecologies of experience, with opinions and beliefs considered as extreme and even insane in each, do co-exist, as definers of Hochschild's 'social terrains', above.

The world isn't just personalised for us and brought to us. It also involves the global expansion of us, our centrality, our global digitalphagia and consumption of the world, our erasure of that-which-is-not-us-in-the-world, to leave a condensed world of information, or rather self-information; a world irradiated by the core that defines our age, the core of self and identity.

## You Can't Fact-Check Reality

We have argued that it was the global, societal and personal revolution in information technology and information, which unleashed the rage that helped smash the existing mainstream news media order. The sudden digital tsunami of billions of images, videos, messages, comments, opinions and claims demanded some kind of dam, something to grasp onto, that was recognisable as safe ground. This over-production of media at scale was characterised by a new availability and visibility of sorts, including a shared exposure to the worst of humanity. Social media platforms that enabled the production, sharing and seeing of the toxic sludge, once smoothed over and pushed out of sight by the mainstream media, were forced to be seen to act. This involved the creation of new rules and systems, including the employment of humans to watch, sift and sanitise the worst of horror, so you don't have to.

More recently, the spread of the AI generation or processing of such material has required a new human army of screening (Hoskins, 2024). There is now a history of debate on the nature, effectiveness, and merits or otherwise of so-called content moderation, seen as pivotal to the relationship between media regulation, national and international law, and privacy and freedom (Young, 2021).

But the MSM response to the digital free-for-all that was disassembling its business model was to call out 'fake news' as the spectre that it could be seen to exercise. President Trump, they believed, offered something that news was never about to protect, namely *truth*, and their weapon—*fact-checking*.

Although initially the work of activists and media NGOs, Trump's first election spawned the institutionalisation of fact-checking through news organisations (including The New York Times, the BBC and the UK's Guardian). By 2016, there were at least 113 such groups, with more than 90% of these being established since 2010, and 50 being launched in the prior two years alone (Graves & Cherubini, 2016). In March 2017, the UK's Channel 4 News advertised for a 'FactCheck Journalist' in March to join its 'award-winning FactCheck team'. The advert read: 'In this era of fake news, post-truth politics and increasingly polarised debate, the work of the team has never been more crucial – and it is expanding as a result[13]'.

But how many fact-checkers does it take to show the President of the US is a liar, or to make news true? Clay Shirky, for instance, highlights the mismatch between this response and the phenomenon it supposedly addresses: 'We've brought fact-checkers to a culture war[14]'. And relatedly, Shirky responds to a tweet that refers to the rapid 'muddying of the waters over the term 'fake news'': 'Those waters were never clear; 'news' is not a stable category. What we had was organizational stability, which we confused with truth'.[15]

News has—in fact—for a long time been forged by opinion, rather than by truth. This should be an obvious outcome to anyone who has tried any fact-checking. For example, one Guardian report highlights the work of Daniel Dale of the Toronto Star, who as the first Trump election campaign progressed spent night after night fact-checking the then presidential candidate, identifying 560 false Trump statements between 15 September and 8 November 2016: 'Despite his own extraordinary late-night efforts; despite the similarly herculean efforts of the New York Times, which dedicated 18 journalists to fact-checking the TV debates in real time, or of NPR, which turned over 30 staffers to a similar endeavor; despite the Guardian's Lyin' Trump column and so much more, some 61 million Americans were unfazed enough by the idea of a serial liar in the Oval Office to vote for him' (Pilkington, 2016).

In a sharded media system in which truth is splintered, rather than shared, fake news has become just another phrase to troll back at those who nostalgically still try and champion twentieth-century imaginaries of the MSM as arbiters of what is true or not. If truth depends on which reality shard you inhabit, then what can fact-checking change? Many of the activists and others who are devoting their energies to fact-checking may well be well-intentioned, but their efforts are not, ultimately, going to render some kind of shared accountability.

Fact-checking seems aimed at a pure vision of something that was never in news in the first place, rather than grasping the means through which sharded media affords acceptability, credibility or legitimacy to its insular prism of events. For example, Benkler et al. (2017) found that: 'Rather than "fake news" in the sense of wholly fabricated falsities, many of the most-shared stories can more accurately be understood as disinformation: the purposeful construction of true or partly true bits of information into a message that is, at its core, misleading'. The tsunami of content has hybridised opinion and propaganda, with virality and contagion as principal forces of legitimacy. Under these conditions, to try to hold up this or that element of news as objective or not, or true or not, is lost in a million self-curated shards.

It is no wonder that fact-checking is food for the trolls. With Facebook's plans to promote fact-checking services (Silverman, 2016), an unlikely applicant was Russia Today (RT) with its 'Fakecheck' site' (Waterson, 2017). Those being fact-checked are fact-checking the fact-checkers. The pursuit of what all claim is the truth is ultimately circular and is not a strategy that will ever succeed in transforming the factual basis or otherwise of content swilling in around contemporary media ecologies.

Fact-checking is an idealistic attempt to reestablish a mythical middle ground and to restore credibility to the MSM as an untainted window on the world. Anyway, isn't fact-checking ultimately flawed in its inevitably partial reach, a problem that exists with the moderation of social media platforms, namely of scale and complexity? What of the billions of posts and stories that will never be reviewed, moderated or fact-checked? Who can say if these have more or less weight or influence than those which are deemed as worthy of checking?

This challenge was once a matter of how risk-averse a platform or regulatory organisation was in what was deemed acceptable in the nature and extent of all the toxic waste it did not or could not catch and filter out. But scale and black box complexity ultimately muted the legitimacy of moderating efforts in the digital era, and which are now utterly defining of AI-sharded experiences and archives, creating 'a past that never existed' (Hoskins, 2024). How can AI-generated news be fact-checked?

The wider point here as to the futility of attempts to de-legitimise or hold the Trump presidency to account is that no amount of fact-checking will shift the sharded views of those who believe (or don't care about) misinformation or disinformation in the first place. Moreover, research by Nyhan and Reifler (2010) reveals a 'backfire effect' whereby facts offered to challenge misinformation believed true even have the effect of reinforcing ideologically founded beliefs. Thus, as Bridges (2017) puts it: 'fighting the ill-informed with facts is like fighting a grease fire with water. It seems like it should work, but it's actually going to make things worse'. Furthermore, as Sarah Oates (2024) concludes in her 2024 US election analysis, 'We may never be able to return to a time when mere facts can compete with imagined desires'.

There was certainly not a shortage of MSM-led investment in fact-checking Trump's first term in office. The Washington Post, for example, developed its own 'Fact Checker' database, which claimed that in this period, 'President Trump made 30,573 false or misleading claims' (Washington Post, 2021).

Despite Bridges' insight (above) that fact-checking is counterproductive, the fact-checking industry proliferated, with organisations and projects spreading to over 100 countries, although by 2024 their number had plateaued (Stencel et al., 2024). Following Trump's re-election, the Washington Post's Glenn Kessler (2024) published an article: 'What I've learned from 9 years of fact-checking Donald Trump'. Kessler reflected on his writing following Trump's defeat in 2020: 'my analysis carried a headline that is embarrassing in retrospect: "Fact-checking in a post-Trump era." I wrote that "his defeat by Democrat Joe Biden suggests that adherence to the facts does matter"' (Kessler, 2024). Ultimately, for Kessler, fact-checking is about informing publics: 'I do not write fact checks to influence the behavior of politicians; I write fact checks to inform voters. What voters — or politicians — do with the information in the fact checks is up to them' (Kessler, 2024).

In one way, this MSM fact-checker's claim that politicians' 'adherence to facts' no longer matters is an extraordinary claim, but in another way, seems fair comment on how much the media ground has shifted between Trump's two election victories. But informing voters as a core function (and anti-fake news strategy) of the MSM is not a sufficient response to be left with for penetrating the sharded media ecologies of the individual.

This MSM adjustment to the new reality was always going to be challenging as they were so effectively targeted as part of the right's weaponisation of populist anti-establishment sentiment. In the digital era of so-called free content, and not least in a 'postphotographic age' (Kennedy, 2015) in which everyone became a media producer, a key MSM survival strategy was to shift from production to the verification of content. The MSM brands of Reuters, BBC, CNN, New York Times and so on, attempted to at least bring the chaos of user-generated content under their wings, through badging it, taming it, authorising it, as ways of reinstating themselves as institutions of trust. Today we are witnessing a similarly flawed approach in the 'watermarking' of AI-generated content.

Following Trump's first election victory, there was still a liberal MSM belief that his supporters had been misled or duped by the ascendent right-wing media, especially by news outlets not shy in their political advocacy such as Fox News, Breibart and Drudge. The playing field was seen as tipped against the liberal MSM in its adherence to any kind of news value (above) that involved the pursuit of impartiality or balance in reporting. Following the publication of research showing the influence of a new right-wing media ecology in the 2016 election, a piece on Breibart's site poked fun at this realisation on the left:

> Clearly unfamiliar with the concept of irony, left-wing Columbia Journalism Review claims that right-wing media led by Breitbart, practices "disinformation" and creates an "insulated knowledge community…" The authors of the study, who were funded by the Open Society Foundation, the Bill & Melinda Gates Foundation, the Robert Woods Foundation, and the Ford Foundation, are not happy about the rise of anti-establishment media. Imagine that! (Bokhari, 2017)

Some liberal mainstream commentators in the wake of Trump's first election asked how they could build a media ecology to match that of the new right. In a Columbia Journalism Review essay entitled 'Creating a Fox News for the left', Hertsgaard (2017) refers to Bill Moyers' warning of the potential for Fox with its Murdoch finances and the skills of Roger Ailes to 'transform the US media and political landscape by distributing well-produced if journalistically fraudulent "news" to vast numbers of Americans'. Moyers and Hertsgaard advocate in response, respectively, a 'truth-telling journalism', that brings audiences 'as close as possible to the verifiable truth' (Hertsgaard, 2017).

But truth-telling does not blunt rage. As Hochschild found in her ethnography, Fox News was one of the principal mediators if not stirrers of this state: 'As a powerful influence over the views of the people I came to know, Fox News stands next to industry, state government, church, and the regular media as an extra pillar of political culture all its own… Fox…suggests what the issues are, It tells her [respondent] what to feel afraid, angry, and anxious about' (2017: 126). This sense of the rage of the disenfranchised is not new in itself, but rather it has found a new powerful mode of expression in Trump's first election and in the UK, the referendum vote to leave the European Union (Brexit). For example, as Mishra (2017: 346) argues 'with the victory of Donald Trump it has become impossible to deny or obscure the great chasm, first explored by Rousseau, between an elite that seizes modernity's choicest fruits while disdaining older truths and uprooted masses, who, on finding themselves cheated of the same fruits, recoil into cultural supremacism, populism and rancorous brutality'. This, Mishra sees as part of a new 'age of anger' (2017). Thus, the rage of the right at what they saw as disenfranchisement by and from the liberal mainstream and its associated establishment institutions rode easily through the emergent digital attention economy of the day.

In the UK, also in 2017, the BBC launched its own 'permanent' 'Reality Check' team, with James Harding its news chief, telling his staff that the corporation would be 'weighing in on the battle over lies, distortions and exaggerations' (Jackson, 2017). In 2023, the BBC appeared to drop this Reality Check label and launched a 'new brand' called BBC Verify, bringing together 60 journalists who will 'be fact-checking, verifying video, countering disinformation, analysing data and, crucially, explaining complex stories in the pursuit of truth (Turness, 2023). The key shift here in the BBC's attempt to acquire trust is through, as they explain, Verify's 'transparently sharing their evidence-gathering with our audiences' (Turness, 2023).

In so doing, the BBC exposes its need to be seen to be shoring up its brand, no longer sufficiently trustworthy for it to just make news. As the journalist, Mary Dejevsky posted on X, '#BBCVerify was a thoroughly bad idea, not least b/c, by implication, it suggests accuracy of even BBC reports needs to be 'verified'. When I was at #BushHouse many moons ago, a #BBC correspondent's word was the gold standard'.[16] But by the run into the 2024 presidential election, a new reality warping and splintering force—artificial intelligence and related technologies and services—had entered the battleground. It is to this latest sharding of truth and trust that we now turn to address.

## AI's Sharding

The liberal MSM made facts and truth their USP, their core pitch for trust, in precisely the period when they became most elusive. Rapid advances in generative AI[17] enabled any individual to re/create high-quality text, images and audio, based on training data, via easily usable interfaces between human and machine. In the run up to the 2024 election, AI produced and churned synthetic content at new scale, collapsing truth and fiction in new black box media ecologies of impossible provenance. Trump's campaign appropriated this final sharding of the media in two interrelated ways.

The first is in their deploying fake or deepfake generative AI images and videos. This includes the rapid production of high resolution, photorealistic visuals, readily insertable, viral and reprogrammable in digital feeds. In March 2023, deepfake images of Trump being arrested were sucked up into visual vortexes, including one shared by Trump on Truth Social of his kneeling and praying. This was just prior to Trump being indicted over hush money payment made to the adult film star Stormy Daniels, who claimed she had an affair with him (Katersky et al., 2023). The praying photo was classic Trump premediation (Grusin, 2004; Hoskins & Loughlin, 2009) of his impending actual arrest, powerfully feeding the narrative of a conspiracy-driven witch hunt against him (see Chapter 3, below).

Meanwhile, leading up to Trump's apron-donned McDonald's photo-shoot in Pennsylvania, his followers, news organisations and even T-shirt sellers used Gen-AI-produced images to mock up what this scene might look like (Warzel, 2024b). Here we have a premediation of an event through a million shards.

The second sharding of media can be seen through the wider production and consumption of 'AI slop'. This is not content that is outrageously wrong, but rather that which is 'subtly wrong' such as 'careless speech', and AI-generated 'news' (Adami, 2024; Wachter et al., 2024), flooding the internet, including publishing platforms such as Medium (Knibbs, 2024). AI slop is a boon for the sharding of reality as it feeds the personal production of the real, the exponential hyper-production of truths, that we call hyporeality (see Chapter 2, below). Warzel (2024b) offers a useful account:

> *Slop* isn't necessarily a commentary on quality so much as on how it is meant to be consumed: fleetingly, and with little or no thought beyond the initial limbic-system response. The main characteristic of slop is that there is an endless supply of it. And so it makes sense that campaigns—not just Trump's—tend to traffic in it. Campaigns are nothing if not aggressive, often-desperate content farms hoping to get attention. In service of that mission, they meme, pander, email, and text, frequently in cringe-worthy fashion. Not unlike the fast food that Trump was hawking, slop is sometimes delicious, but it is never nutrient dense.

In an environment defined by so much AI-generated content slopping around, it becomes easier to call out anything and everything as suspect, as with Trump's trolling of his 2024 opponent, Kamala Harris. On the 24 August, he posted on Truth Social: 'Has anyone noticed that Kamala CHEATED at the airport? There was nobody at the plane, and she "A.I.'d" it, and showed a massive "crowd" of so-called followers, BUT THEY DIDN'T EXIST!'.[18]

Predictably, the MSM accelerated attention to this one posting, reporting it as a false claim, including by the AFP Fact Check service (B. McCarthy, 2024). In this war, we return to Jarvis' (2016) question (above), 'what is an appropriate journalistic strategy in a gaslit political world? Reporting on method over message? Selective silence?' Almost a decade later, this is not an approach that has been implemented. Rather, the MSM have become more entrenched in their response to a torrent of AI-image generation of increasingly realistic images and videos, to find ways to expose them as fake, as untrue (Bond, 2023; Devlin & Cheetham, 2023).

As with the development of fact-checking (above), with each new form of production and manipulation of message, image and video, the MSM instinct is to try and show these as synthetic, compared with their own branded truth. The period between Trump's elections is marked by the *layering* of mechanisms, technologies and media literacies, to this end.

But this ever more frantic search for their former singular mainstream reality is ultimately fruitless amidst the millions of sharded other realities, today in AI-rendered individual feeds. As we have argued, throwing moderators, fact-checkers and verifiers, at a self-righteous pursuit of an MSM-badged truth, is a catastrophic misidentification of the problem.

The sharding of experience through smartphones, apps, messaging, personal networks, favoured platforms, recommendations and peer-linked sources shapes an everyday political awareness, experience and activity, much of which is humorous, satirical, irreverent and sarcastic: lampooning, ridiculing and parodying political opposition. Trolling makes journalistic-based solutions redundant as the MSM is alienated from the very infrastructure it depends upon for its existence. But generative AI is the ultimate troll weapon, sharding much more instant and vivid truths, an irresistible fusion of the hyporeal.

In our next chapter (2), we develop this argument to show how the rapid and easy production of personally curated information has sharded the shared, mass-mediated understanding of the world into individual realities. This fragmentation, fuelled by personalised algorithms and the proliferation of conspiracies, forges hyporeality in which personal belief trumps the weight of evidence.

In Chapter 3, we show how Trump's entire politics are based on a kind of pornographic *self-over-exposure* of his personality and views, a collapsing of his front stage and back stage. This enables him to reflect and to carry the rage and frustration felt by many voters alienated by established political systems.

Chapter 4 develops our argument that Trump's 2024 victory harnessed public rage at a government seemingly captured by an array of elites, including professional politicians, MSM, 'metropolitans', the 'deep state', global corporations and the super-rich.

Following this, Chapter 5 maps the shift of the technology elite from supporting liberal values, as espoused by the early Silicon Valley, to openly aligning with the populist right. This new alliance of the broligarchy leverages technology and anti-democratic sentiments to further its goals. Trump's support is forged through a paradoxical coalition of disenfranchised voters seeking re-entry into a more responsive government, and a radicalised elite seeking a total exit from all state control and democratic governance.

In Chapter 6, we conclude on how the digital reversal of the democratic principles of collectivity and compromise results in zombie capitalism. This is a system that is undead, rotting and driven by a relentless, unthinking rage, much like the modern zombie of popular culture.

## NOTES

1. *Network* (1976) directed by Sidney Lumet, written by Paddy Chayefsky.
2. Ibid.
3. The Voice of America (VOA) is the oldest and largest US government-funded international media organization. See Kate Wright's (2024) Bluesky thread following Trump's appointment of Kari Lake to head the VOA, 12th December, https://bsky.app/profile/newsprof1.bsky.social/post/3ld47kwkze22f.
4. See Catherine Happer's (2024) superb work on public opinion and trust in a digital age.
5. The term 'artificial intelligence' (AI) many trace to the US computer scientist John McCarthy (1927–2011) and his 1955 definition of AI as 'the science and engineering of making intelligent

machines, especially intelligent computer programs' (McCarthy 2007).

6. Screenshot of Google Books Ngram Viewer with entry 'media crisis' in range 1920–2022, https://books.google.com/ngrams/graph?content=media+crisis&year_start=1920&year_end=2022&corpus=en&smoothing=3.

7. Jeff Jarvis @jeffjarvis, Twitter, 9th November 2016.

8. Jeff Jarvis @jeffjarvis and Jay Rosen @jayrosen Twitter exchange, 24th August 2017.

9. Jay Rosen @jayrosen, X, 8th November 2024, https://x.com/jayrosen_nyu/status/1855023143896985736.

10. Carol Cadwalladr, @carolecadwalla.bsky.social, BlueSky, 17th November 2024, https://bsky.app/profile/carolecadwalla.bsky.social/post/3lb575efhtx2n.

11. https://www.instagram.com/thefreepress/reel/DA6ZG5aCmqR/.

12. Jeff Jarvis @jeffjarvis, X, 17th December 2024, https://x.com/jeffjarvis/status/1869122223698743695.

13. FactCheck Journalist, Channel 4 News, *The Guardian* jobs: https://jobs.theguardian.com/job/6479268/factcheck-journalist-channel-4-news/?LinkSource=PremiumListing (March 2017, link no longer available).

14. Clay Shirky @cshirky, Twitter, 22nd July 2016, https://twitter.com/cshirky/status/756569741020377088.

15. Clay Shirky @cshirky, Twitter, 16th December 2016, https://twitter.com/cshirky/status/809634747932549120.

16. Mary Dejevsky, @marydejevsky, X, 4th March 2024, https://x.com/marydejevsky/status/1764689277491757124.

17. Examples of generative AI include: Open AI's Chat GPT, Google's Gemini (formerly Bard) and Meta's Llama 3. OpenAI's, DALL-E2 and Stability AI's Stable Diffusion are specifically developed for generating images and art from text prompts.

18. Donald J. Trump @realDonaldTrump, TruthSocial, 11th August 2024, https://truthsocial.com/@realDonaldTrump/posts/112944255426268462.

# CHAPTER 2

# Donald Trump and the Sharding of the Real

**Abstract** Sharded media have produced a state of hyporeality, in which easily produced and personally curated information diminishes the attainment and significance of a shared, objective truth. The digital revolution has unleashed personal realities and individualised experience, forced upon us a much more complex process of sense-making and hyper-inflating our own voice and our own important opinions, all of which we try to force back upon the world. This chapter, instead of following the trend to see conspiracy theorists as somehow fundamentally different and deluded, argues rather that they are *like us*. Contrary to the Democrat's never-Trumpism and Kamala Harris' late-campaign rhetoric warning of Trump's fascism and threat to democracy, for millions of Americans, *in their realities*, it was precisely that 'democracy' was the problem and Trump that was the solution. For many, given the 2020 'steal', *Trump was actually the president* and this was merely the re-election of the incumbent. Hence he could campaign as simultaneously the real sitting president and as an outsider who would have run the country better. This chapter turns over the perception that others are trapped in unreal and deluded states, but rather is a result of the sharding of a broadcast era mass-consensual reality.

**Keywords** Hyporeality · Truth · Post-truth · Filter bubble · Mainstream bubble · Conspiracy theory · Epistemological war · Covid-19 pandemic

In November 2016, the US public elected as president a celebrity-businessman, cameo film-actor, member of the WWE Hall of Fame and Reality-TV host who had never held any public office. Donald Trump defeated one of the best-qualified presidential candidates in living memory to take the White House. In 2020, however, all of this seemed to be reversed. Trump's disastrous handling of Covid-19, his erratic opinions and actions and their impact on the economy led to his defeat by the Democrats. His subsequent encouragement of a MAGA march on the capital on 6th January 2021 and incitement of a violent populist attempt to overthrow the US democratic process seemed to finally put Trump beyond political acceptability. The feeling among many was that, with Biden's victory, normal politics and normal service had been resumed. The disintegration of QAnon and the Republican's poor showing in the 2022 mid-terms, where a hoped-for 'red-wave' failed to materialise, seemed to suggest that MAGA's public and electoral appeal had definitively dimmed. The Trumpian interregnum was over, with Trump himself reduced to a churlish, public fight for his liberty and reputation against a series of lawsuits.

Then, on 5th November 2024, the US public re-elected Donald Trump as president. This time they had chosen a convicted felon, guilty of 34 counts of violating a New York law on corporate record-keeping who was also facing (or had faced) three other lawsuits, including a federal election interference case, claimed electoral interference in Georgia and charges regarding the taking of sensitive national security documents to his Mar-a-Lago resort and the prevention of their retrieval (Politico, 2024). In 2023, he'd already vowed 'retribution' for his personal and his supporter's enemies (Haberman & Goldmacher, 2023) and suggested that, if re-elected, he'd be a dictator from 'day one' (Gold, 2023). His 2024 campaign was marked by incoherent speeches and rambling answers, rampant egoism, lies, distortions, bizarre behaviour, hatred, intimations of violence and the open abuse of ethnic minorities and women. As a direct result of this, he won the popular vote as well as the electoral college, with over 74.6 m votes. For those who'd been following the neck-and-neck polls, the ease of his victory was simply stunning. It was as if the pollsters and commentators had been following a different reality.

Because they had.

Trump himself had long ago taught us that. On 21st January 2017, the day after Trump's first inauguration, images began circulating on social media comparing his crowd's with Obama's in 2009. Compared to the sea of people then, stretching back along the National Mall, Trump's crowd was smaller and patchy. Trump, who never liked having anything seen as smaller than another man's; who'd bragged that his inauguration would have 'an unbelievable, perhaps record-breaking turnout', (PBS, 2017) was rankled. In a speech that day, he claimed to have seen 'a massive field of people … packed' with up to 1.5 m people and hours later his press secretary Sean Spicer accused the media of 'false reporting' and of intentionally framing the photos to minimise the apparent support. 'This was the largest audience ever to witness an inauguration, PERIOD; both in person and around the globe', he angrily declared (Hunt, 2017). Despite the obvious failure to replicate the 1.8 m who'd attended in 2009, the administration doubled down. On the 22nd, Kellyanne Conway, the Counselor to the President, defended Spicer in a *Meet the Press* interview saying, 'Our press secretary, Sean Spicer, gave alternative facts…' (Bradner, 2017).

The phrase was deliberately chosen. It didn't suggest that different interpretations of the world existed, but instead that entire *alternative worlds* existed. It suggested that Trump's crowd *was* bigger and your senses were wrong. Politicians, of course, have always been evasive and given their best spin on contrary evidence, but there were previously limits on deniability. That's why the administration's response was important. This wasn't simply about spin or even lying—instead they went on the offensive, challenging people to look at the images for themselves and see what they were told to see. The closest echo was in George Orwell's *1984* when O'Brien interrogates Winston Smith, holding up four fingers and electrocuting him when he doesn't give—*and actually believe*—the answer five. This is what Trump and co. did to the public. They told them what they could actually see, electrocuting the public sphere, torturing the real itself, to make us see and believe what they said. In doing so, they confirmed our passage into the age of hyporeality.

## The Cambrian Explosion of Realities

Looking back today, we can see more clearly the contours of the broadcast era. In the centuries following Johann Gutenberg's invention of mechanical, moveable-type printing, a model developed of the mass-reproduction, mass-distribution and mass-consumption of information. By the twentieth century, this had evolved into huge structures of communication producing messages: into corporations and public organisations employing large numbers in vast industries—print, radio, music, cinema, television—organised in a factory system to produce standardised, uniform content. It was a world of 'big media', of top-down, one-to-many production, pushing out vast quantities of media products at receptive audiences. But this wasn't just about the provision of entertainment. What was being mass-produced was *reality* itself.

It was a point well understood by thinkers such as Daniel Boorstin (1992), Guy Debord (1977) and Jean Baudrillard. What they agreed upon was that the broadcast media were primarily *epistemological engines*, creating our experience, knowledge, concepts of truth and horizons of thought. Baudrillard's early work on the post-war semiotic, consumer societies, for example, explored how electronic mass media transform 'the lived, eventual character of the world' into signs that are combined to produce the real (Baudrillard, 1998: 123). 'Over the whole span of daily life', he says, 'a vast process of simulation is taking place', with the semiotic media assuming 'the force of reality', obliterating the real in favour of its own model (1998: 126). The media modelled and presented an efficacious reality.

For Baudrillard, what increasingly characterised these media-produced 'simulacra' was their 'hyperreality'—their excessive, close-up, high-definition and 'pornographic' technical semio-realisation of the real (1990a: 11, 50). By the late 1970s to early 1980s, Baudrillard had grown to see this *excess* as central to our system. This is a culture, he argues, devoted to 'production'—understood not as industrial manufacture, but in the original sense of 'to render visible, to cause to appear and be made to appear: *pro-ducere*' (1987: 21). Hence his furious description of our entire *productive society*—our 'orgy of realism', our 'rage ... to summon everything before the jurisdiction of signs', to make everything visible, legible, rendered, recorded and available, with everything passing over into 'the absolute evidence of the real' (1990b: 32, 32, 29). Ours, he says, 'is a pornographic culture par excellence' (1990b: 34).

Though Baudrillard died in March 2007, on the cusp of the release of the iPhone and the take-off of Web 2.0, and though much of his work described the world of electronic mass media, there is one way in which he may be one of the key thinkers of the age of social media: because the digital revolution represents the continuation of that *society of production* he describes. This was a theme continued throughout his work. His

**2004** book *The Intelligence of Evil* returned to the Western drive for 'integral reality', explained as 'the perpetuating on the world of an unlimited operational project whereby everything becomes real, everything becomes visible and transparent, everything is "liberated", everything comes to fruition and has a meaning' (Baudrillard, 2005: 17). The digital revolution, therefore, represents the extension of this process, achieving the final liberation—that of production itself.

We will, one day, find it remarkable that for centuries, during the Gutenbergian broadcast era, we limited the ability to produce and share the real. For so long you needed permission, licenses, skills, qualifications, employment, key positions within communicational hierarchies and expensive and complex equipment, etc., before you were able to create and share information. There were, of course, options for individual production, but the tools (typewriter, photocopier, 8 mm, polaroids) were limited, distribution was difficult and there was little cultural interest in amateur creation. For centuries, it was an elite of professional creators that made our real. What the digital revolution accomplished was the liberation of the power of production and distribution. Now anyone with a smartphone became an empowered producer of content, messages and information (Merrin, 2014).

As smartphone possession has increased—by June 2024, there were 7.2 bn smartphones in the world, covering around 90% of the world's population with over 10.47 bn mobile connections (Howarth, 2024)—so too has the personal production of the real. Using an array of devices, technologies, apps, platforms, services and software, we now devote ourselves daily to the recording of our lives, experiences, movements and thoughts, in a *self-paparizzization* for our friends, families and subscribed global followers.

In retrospect, therefore the entire broadcast era looks like a decidedly amateur project, with only a tiny minority devoted to the real's production. In contrast, digitality crowd-sources that project to us all. One day we'll look back with horror at how much of the real went unrecorded and how much we allowed to disappear. Now, in theory, there isn't a single moment, activity, relationship, personal body-part or experience that escapes potential capture and the possibility of being added to the pornographic hyper-visible, hyper-intimate, personally-archived collection of the museum of the real.

One of the key ideas Baudrillard takes from media theorist Marshall McLuhan is 'reversal'—the idea that at 'the peak of performance' technologies can reverse their effects (McLuhan, 1994: 30, 33, 182). The same process can be seen with our production of the real. Following the economic law that over-production leads to devaluation, so our devotion to the over-production of the real leads to a crash in its stocks. We move from the excessive hyperreality of the broadcast era—where huge organisations gathered and deployed vast stocks of *media materiel* to create the real—to a digital world of personally produced *hyporeality*, where the personal production of the real is inflated and the real as a shared experience deflates. If broadcast hyperreality was marked by excess, then our digital hyporeality ('hypo', meaning 'under' or 'less') is marked by decline and loss. For when the weight of the real comes down to the self and its productions, then little or nothing is required to create it, to claim it or to believe in it. Just as hyperreality was an ongoing process—that of the accumulation and perfection of the real—then so too is hyporeality, representing the real's reversive, spiralling decline.

This argument chimes with the claimed contemporary crisis of 'truth'. In recent years, fears of online disinformation, 'fake news', state-trolling and conspiracy theorism have led some to argue we live in a 'post-truth' world (Ball, 2018; D'Ancona, 2017; Davis, 2017; Fuller, 2018; Kakutani, 2018; McIntyre, 2018). One explanation for this crisis is Eli Pariser's idea that today we are locked into personalised, online 'filter bubbles', created by our own curation of our networks and information and by algorithms feeding us more of what we like to increase our engagement (Pariser, 2011). This idea has merit but it's worth expanding upon it and projecting the concept backwards. For then, we can understand that these personal bubbles are predicated upon the earlier existence of a single, all-encompassing bubble.

Because the entire world of broadcast mass media formed *a mainstream bubble*; one producing, for its inhabitants, a complete, enclosed, self-sufficient, self-referencing and self-reinforcing world of news, information and entertainment. It formed an entire *reality*, albeit it one carefully and collectively filtering the world. These filters included the use of market demographics for product-targeting, professional codes of conduct, government licensing and regulation of producers, and the broadcaster's need to retain the goodwill of advertisers and consumers. A careful restriction of production and content ensured nothing dangerous, extreme, offensive or too different ever appeared. Even nudity was rare in the mainstream. The 'Goatse', 'Two Girls One Cup', ISIS beheadings and white supremacist propaganda would never appear in its broadcasts.

Digital technologies transformed the entire structure of societal communication. They liberated production and distribution, empowering every individual and unleashing the full spectrum of voices, ideas and opinions. As well as tipping older industries into economic crisis, they also challenged the cultural and political dominance of mainstream outlets as it became clear the public were as interested in—indeed, were *more* interested in—their own and others' voices as anything the broadcast media had to say. In a radical reversal, a 'like', a comment, a gif-reaction, a TikTok video, snapchat filter, message or meme could mean more to someone than a big-budget, star-powered, Hollywood CGI-fest, years in the making. It was about what you personally wanted. The world of broadcast media gave way to the radically personally-centred and personalised world of *me-dia* (Merrin, 2014: 77–92). And as a result, digital technologies exploded our informational sources into the fractal fragments of everything we could see or find—every friend, follower, message, DM, link, web page, forum thread, post, comment, group chat, gif, meme, photograph, video, 'like' or 'story' and into anything we can think, do, explore and enjoy, however far outside the mainstream.

Hence digital technologies, with their individualised productive, distributive and informational power, burst the simple, unilateral, top-down, mainstream bubble of mass-produced, mass-filtered and mass-consumed, *mass-consensual reality*. As in ecological theory, where a radical change in the food-web of one trophic level has a knock-on effect throughout the other layers in a 'trophic cascade', so digital technologies disrupted the existing epistemological ecology, producing *an extinction cascade of the mainstream real*. This is, therefore, about more than simple 'filter bubbles': the explosion of the mainstream reality-bubble has created an infinite body of *individual, monadic bubbles*. Except they are not atomised and separable, they are always in motion, continually connecting and reforming *as foam*: they join and build with other bubbles, to form what Sloterdijk in other circumstances has called 'foam cities'—comprising millions of bubbles which are 'not simply an agglomeration of neighbouring (partition-sharing) inert and massive bodies, but rather multiplicities of loosely touching cells of life-worlds' (Sloterdijk, 2016: 565). And Sloterdijk is right: these are indeed life-worlds, because each of them constitutes its own reality. The explosion of the broadcast era has launched us off on our own, individualised trajectories as tiny, hyperconnected medianauts making and remaking our own worlds.

*This* is the primary effect of the digital revolution and understanding it is the key to understanding politics and public discourse today. In contrast to the nineteenth-century 'Age of Typography' and the twentieth-century 'Age of Television', both of which Neil Postman saw as connecting and unifying their audiences as a shared public (Postman, 1987), what characterises the age of digital media is the radical disconnection from any shared public and mass-consensual reality, except that chosen and created by the self. The foam of bubbles is a foam of personally-created and connected life-worlds.

What we are experiencing, therefore, is *a Cambrian explosion of realities*. The Cambrian explosion is a period of time, around 538 m years ago, when a sudden massive increase in taxonomic life occurred and most of the major animal phyla started appearing in the fossil record. Today, we are experiencing our own explosion—that of reality. Hence the problem is not that we are post-truth or lack truth today. The problem is the opposite: it is the exponential hyper-production of truths. There have never before been so many truths, so many realities. The hyper-equipped, hyper-empowered, hyper-productive hyper-distributed and shared digital self creates their own spin-off reality with every action. Hyporeality— the lowest degree of reality necessary to project or claim or believe anything—rules.

Digital technologies, therefore, have radically decentred *the engines of reality-creation* to each of us and hence we need to properly understand what the 'social' in 'social media' really means. This is not the 'social' of modernity—that 'social' theorised by liberalism, or by Durkheim, Weber or Marx. It is not the contract that founds government, nor the nexus of norms, values and laws, nor the division of labour or the superstructure that arises from it, nor the shared, collective experience of cities and crowds, nor the individual's position within the organic whole, nor the interconnected economic, legal, political, cultural, aesthetic and religious relationship of 'total social facts' (Mauss, 1990: 78–79). Instead, the individual bubbles form their own worlds, continually connecting with others and breaking and reforming these foams on every topic, making worlds out of their own thoughts, interests and networks, replacing the 'social' of modernity with a very different and opposing 'social': the social of *social life*. This a radically, personally-centred network of friends and contacts within their individual life-worlds. With it, the social of modernity is reduced to the zero degree of heat—to the banality of *my social life*, my friends, connections, ideas and opinions.

This has significant implications for 'public discourse'. 'Public' comes to us from the Latin, 'publicus', meaning 'of the people; of the state; done for the state', being derived from the Old Latin 'poplicus', 'pertaining to the people' (from 'populus', meaning 'people'). By late fourteenth-century Europe, the word 'publike' was also being used to refer to that which was 'open to general observation' (Online Etymology Dictionary, 2022). All these meanings point to the collective, the shared bond, the organising institutions and their openness and visibility. And it is these that *our social* threatens.

Because today we live not in the shared, broadcast-era world of top-down communication and authority but instead in personalised bubbles and chosen-foams: in radically individually-curated and created realities. The minor differences in the mainstream broadcast bubble (which newspaper or channel you consumed) have exploded into fractal worlds of informational difference. The moment I wake up and engage with the world, what I open, what I see, what I read and what I share *is utterly unique to me*, as the product of my own choices and algorithmic curation. Little or nothing binds us all today, and, in taking place on platforms and apps and messenger services, much of what we see, consume and share doesn't even count as openly, visibly 'publike'. Do we even have a 'public discourse', therefore, in the age of digital media?

The explosion of the mass-consensual bubble; the extinction cascade of the broadcast ecology of the real; the fractalisation of information; the orbitalised launching of individual medianauts; the blooming of personally-created and connected foam cities: they all point to the splintering of experience and knowledge and reality. Actually, the idea of splinters may, indeed, be useful here. In *Camera Lucida* Roland Barthes, trying to find the secret of photography, claimed images contained a 'punctum', a detail which pierces the individual viewer ('This *something* has triggered me, has provoked a tiny shock, a *sartori*, the passage of a void'). These are personal, remaining different for each viewer. Today's algorithmic feeds and personalised searches return to us a splintered real; one that pierces us, but doesn't necessarily hold anything for any other (Barthes, 1993: 49). Or, perhaps a better concept is that of *sharding*.

In online, multi-player video-games such as *World of Warcraft*, 'sharding' is a game design tool to prevent gamer overcrowding in outdoor areas and improve server performance. At a certain density, the game creates a new 'shard'—a new copy of that area, to allow users to enjoy it without crowding or lag. This new world appears identical to the old and is seamlessly integrated into their experience. Hence gamers can 'live' the same world, the same game-processes, without realising they exist in separate worlds with no possibility of interaction. To all intents and purposes, they are *there*, in the shared world, alongside everyone else, at this point in space and time, but, without them knowing or noticing, their reality is totally separate from and different to those on another sharded server. This is our world today. We each exist in our own sharded, filtered, algorithmically and personally-fed realities. Hence, the dominance of *the feed*—that endless, algorithmically-generated flow of information to us which today has less to do with that TV news tradition of ticker-tape updates underneath the presenter, than it does with *The Matrix*'s vision of a plugged-in pod-humanity being filled and fed by tubes run by an algorithmic artificial intelligence.

Sharded realities. We've barely noticed this, let alone tried to think through what it actually means. Consider war. In 2003, we all sat and watched the live feeds from Iraq ('press the red button for extra content') on the major live news channels. The internet was at an early stage and news websites and some blogs were about as far as we could get without additional language skills or cultural knowledge. We shared the war and watched live as, in the absence of Saddam Hussein, his statue was brought down by celebrating Iraqis, with the help of US troops, and as President Bush declared 'Mission Accomplished' on the USS Abraham Lincoln, moored off the coast of San Diego (Merrin, 2018: 88–105).

Fast-forward to 2022. The mainstream media can barely report the Ukraine War. Even the BBC has now become sharded from the battlefield (the BBC's Ukraine reports came initially live from Kiev, not live from the towns where Russians are killing civilians or live from the main frontlines). The mainstream reporting on Gaza is even worse, failing to capture the horror and destruction. Instead, each of us has our own feed. Soldiers have theirs, and citizen-victims and local populations have theirs too. Governments and military authorities and institutions all have theirs. Each collects or is fed a unique, ever-changing ecology of platforms, sources, videos, claims, posts, comments, propaganda, fakery, disinformation and data.

Each of us, therefore, has our own war and even following or agreeing on what is happening becomes impossible. And everyone has their axe to grind. Just look at the Israel-Hamas War on TikTok and the explosion of biased, propagandist content, all competing to lie, to dissimulate, to beat other narratives, to win with filters, lies, memes, disinfo and creator-opinions. The Hobbesian concept of 'the war of all against all' was, for him, a description of the pure liberty preceding the establishment of society. Today, this is the digital reality of society. We are engaged in an always-on informational battle against everyone with a different opinion, against not a collective, but a new digital multitude. The most visible wars in history are the *least* collectively shared and understood.

Perhaps it's a coincidence that over this exact period the remarkably successful Marvel Cinematic Universe has promoted, throughout its series of interconnected films, the concept of 'the multiverse'—a concept that supposes every action spins off a different timeline and universe, all existing parallel to each other. That infinity of realities has indeed become our life, albeit within our sole universe. Today we all get to choose and explore whatever real we want. Reality itself becomes *a weaponizable concept* against anyone you disagree with. Reality is *yours*: just make it up.

## 'Do Your Research!' The Rise of Conspiracism

Trump's presidency began with one alternative fact—his claim of the largest inauguration crowd ever—and it ended with another: with the claim that he'd won the election. Early on the morning of 4th November 2020, whilst votes were still being counted, Trump suddenly claimed his own votes had been discounted: 'This is a fraud on the American public. This is an embarrassment to this country. We were getting ready to win this election. Frankly, we did win this election' (Smith, 2020b). On the one level this wasn't surprising. Trump had prepared the same claim of fraud in 2016 in case he'd lost and had re-seeded the idea during the 2020 election campaign, whilst the psychology of Trump—a man so obsessed with winning that even servicemen dying in war were 'losers' and 'suckers' (Goldberg, 2020)—couldn't countenance public failure. Hence—mind-flip—he hadn't failed: he'd won.

We can even see the moment that spin-off universe was created, in that instant when Trump went from 'getting ready to win the election' to 'we did win this election'. Trump, the post-modern 'Pere Ubu' of politics (Alfred Jarry's terrifying 1896 image of a grotesque, pulsional dictator, ruling by whim), simply passed from one claim to another, instantly cancelling the former with a new reality. It was so successful a trick, he immediately pulled it again and added an acceptance speech: 'It's a very sad moment to me, a very sad moment, and we are going to win this. As far as I'm concerned, we already have won this, so I want to thank all of our supporters and I want to thank everybody that worked with us'.

There was something god-like here, for the power of the divine has always been the power *to make reality*—to call it into being merely by its declaration. 'In the beginning was the word', *Genesis* declares, and the God who announces 'Let there be light' is talking to no-one (for no-one else yet exists) but is instead making a progenitive demand of existence, of the earth and heavens, tearing a new reality from their being. Speech, for the powerful, is a declarative not a communicative act: it is a statement of what is and must be; a founding of the real that brooks no resistance or debate. In the age of hyporeality, this ancient power has found a new resonance, albeit as a parody of divine power. Because, when Trump declared himself the electoral victor this was, indeed, the founding of a universe, but one manifested *against* the existing order. It was the spin-off of *a bubble universe* within the real. From November 2020, therefore, Americans lived in two simultaneous and opposing realities: one where Trump remained president and another where he'd lost.

The culmination of this force of will was the 6th January 2021 storming of the US Capitol building in Washington DC. The armed protest, and the violence, was openly organised over social media, on 4Chan and TheDonald.win and on messaging apps such as Parler and Telegram. The day began with speeches at the Washington monument, with Rudy Giuliani calling for 'trial by combat' and Trump declaring 'if you don't fight like hell, you're not going to have a country anymore' (Savage, 2021). At 1 pm, the crowds began to march to the Capitol building where they breached the barriers, broke inside, fought with Capitol police officers and hunted down politicians to kill. The protestors were an alliance of online-inspired MAGA Trumpists, 'patriots', QAnons, militia members such as the Proud Boys, white supremacists (with their Confederate imagery), the 'Groyper Army', the 'Boogaloo bois', Alt-Righters, 4Chan anons (carrying Kekistan flags) and neo-Nazis (with 'Camp Auschwitz' and 6MNE—'6 million not enough'—t-shirts). Inspired by *The Turner Diaries'* vision of 'The Day of the Rope', they also constructed a gallows outside the building. 'Murder the media' was graffitied in the building, news-crews were attacked outside and police were beaten, with one killed and over 50 injured. Three pipe-bomb IEDs were also found in different locations.

This was simultaneously a real, armed political insurrection and an internet-inspired, selfie-taking, *cos-play festival*, delighting in the destruction, the ransacking of the enemy-state and the looting of its symbols. Trump's first, reluctant, video-message call to step-down turned into a statement of support—'We love you, you're very special'—before an evening statement and Twitter video message on the 7th backtracked, dissociating himself from his supporters. For some, this was evidence of deep-state deep fakery, though others were disappointed by Trump's lack of support, especially when, in the following months, they were traced and arrested. Nevertheless, the threat from these supporters remained real. In their bubble universe, Trump was still the president. This was the product of the dominance today—for all of us—of conspiracy theorism.

Conspiracy theorism has a long history, as does its effects, with hoax texts such as the *Protocols of the Elders of Zion* continuing to shape contemporary politics. Most theories, however, had a more limited purchase as broadcast-era filters prevented the publication or stocking of extreme ideas, whilst the rest was a niche interest, filed in shops and libraries alongside cryptozoology, ghosts and UFOs. Ultimately, what conspiracy theorists lacked were *friends*. Hence the internet's transformative effect in allowing easy publication, linking to other pages and conspiracies, and enabling like-minded people to find each other, to communicate and share ideas as a community. Where conspiracist ideas did manage to affect the mainstream, for example with Holocaust denialism, systems of truth put them in their place. Deborah Lipstadt and Penguin Books' 2000, evidence based, legal demolition of the Holocaust denier David Irving's defamation suit against them was seen at the time as sounding the death knell of denialism (Lipstadt, 2005). It wasn't. Soon after, Web 2.0 exploded and after that you didn't need to be a 'historian' with a book contract to publish denialism: now anyone with an internet connection could make it up whilst sitting in their bedroom.

Whereas many 1960s–70s conspiracy theories appealed to the left in their countercultural suspicion of the state and 'the man', by the 1990s conspiracy theorism had drifted to the right, accelerating during the Clinton presidency and, again, through Obama's. By then they'd bloomed: 9/11 as a Jewish plot, or false-flag, the 'birther' conspiracy, immigration as a Democrat plot, multiculturalism as planned genocide, chem-trail population control, climate change denialism, FEMA concentration camps readied for the population and belief in an elite 'New World

Order'. Radio shock-jocks, hyper-partisan news and conspiracy celebrities such as Alex Jones and the UK's David Icke all pushed these ideas, with Jones' Infowars even interviewing the 'birther', future-conspiracy-theorist-in-chief Donald Trump in December 2015.

Alt-right conspiracies helped propel Trump to power, but the most successful pro-Trump theory was 'QAnon', which emerged in October 2017. There was little here that was new, in revisiting historical anti-Semitism, revitalising #pizzagate and the hatred of Hilary Clinton, drawing in human-trafficking threads, employing a typical LARP-insidership persona and pushing predictable alt-right/MAGA politics, but, thanks to two 4Chan moderators and a YouTuber, the idea spread to the broader net. Exploiting public fears of child-exploitation, happily absorbing other conspiracies and pushed by social media recommendation engines, QAnon morphed into a vast, international meta-conspiracy. Even British grannies on Facebook, with no interest in Trump, pushed the #Savethechildren campaign and marched under its banner. In the US, two Republican QAnons were elected to Congress in November 2020 (see Badham, 2022; Ball, 2023; Bloom & Moskalenko, 2021; Rothschild, 2021; Sommer, 2023).

QAnon represented the realisation of internet conspiracism, not only in using it to spread, but as a creation of the medium, exploiting its affordances. The actual content of the theory was less ludicrous than the idea that Trump knew what he was doing and was organising everything from behind the scenes. What mattered, however, was the ludic pleasure of digital conspiracising. Because QAnon was a product of Web 2.0: it was a democratised, participatory phenomenon, allowing everyone to join in and add to it. It was an alternative reality game, imploding the internet and real-life (RL), with a self-reinforcing, collaborative community pursuing online and real-world 'clues' to inflate an alternative, Trumpist, bubble universe, *alternative reality*. QAnon was both immersive in drawing in and trapping people within its mythos, and empowering, in exploiting discontent with mainstream media (MSM) messages and pushing instead individual investigation with a slogan that was simultaneously exhortative for insiders and accusatory for outsiders: 'Do your research!' 'Research' here became a hyper-paranoid, Google-based, radical symptomology of the real, with the initiated discovering and deciphering the secret-signs of the political world, explaining away failures and dead-drops within the accepted bubble-narrative. Reality itself was *gamified*.

With lockdown keeping people indoors and online, many found themselves drawn to QAnon. It became an endlessly metastasising meta-conspiracy, linking to and ingesting everything else. For adherents it became a *deep truth*, definitively separating oneself from the MSM and its reality, locking followers into a gnostic theology of good patriots and defenders of children vs evil elites, with an eschatological vision of a coming retributive end-of-days and a cultic fervour that brooked no dissent. Trump's claims of victory kept the bubble universe alive in the aftermath of his defeat and its exposure.

The pandemic allowed other conspiracy theories to thrive. The enforced lockdown appeared as the long awaited, spectacular proof of the state's plans for control. Covid-19 conspiracies erupted, multiplied, intersected and morphed, bringing different groups and fears into contact. The most common claim was that Covid-19 was a 'hoax'—it was no more dangerous than flu; it was a state plan to remove our freedoms; it was man-made in the lab; it was deliberately created to peddle Big Pharma's ready-made vaccine cures; it was created in order to force vaccinations upon us; it was financed by a global elite, including Bill Gates and George Soros, in alliance with Big Pharma, to make huge profits. Or it was a Chinese lab-leak; or a Chinese-made bioweapon; or Covid-19 was just a cover-story for the cancer-causing properties of 5G. 5G tower radiation, it was claimed, sucked oxygen from the atmosphere, hence people's inability to breathe, with its shortwave radiation breaking down our natural biology. Or vaccination was a plot by Bill Gates to inject 5G nano-technology mind-control and tracking chips or rewrite our DNA. The World Economic Forum leader Klaus Schwab's handy publication of a book entitled *The Great Reset* in July 2020 (Schwab & Malleret, 2020) about the possibility of using the pandemic to remake the world sent the conspiracy theorists into uncontrollable conniptions. Amazon was soon flooded with self-published books by conspiracy theorists with similar titles.

Conspiracy theorist coronavirus opposition increased. Rule breaking was common, with non-mask wearing becoming a libertarian statement of principle to be defended with violence. Anti-lockdown marches merged with anti-vaccination, anti-mask, anti-5G, anti-elite, anti-paedophile and anti-child-trafficking sentiments. One anti-vaccine leaflet depicted Auschwitz with an entrance sign reading 'Vaccines are safe path to freedom' (Quinn, 2021). In the UK, a dedicated subculture appealing to the Magna Carta to override state Covid-19 regulations emerged (Coleman,

2021); conspiracy theorists broke into hospitals to post videos of empty corridors and wards to expose the hoax (Giles et al., 2021), and a nurse, Kate Shemirani, became one of the leading anti-Covid-19 and anti-vaccination spokespeople, claiming NHS staff would 'stand trial for genocide' (Hancock, 2021). In Iran, one cleric claimed the vaccine made you homosexual (O'Neill, 2021).

With the pandemic's appearance, existing conspiracy theories were updated, with Alex Jones, David Icke and QAnon joining in, whilst celebrities such as Lewis Hamilton, Madonna and Naomi Wolff pushed coronavirus and vaccine misinformation. Social platforms were forced into an escalating war against the conspiracy theorist 'infodemic', with Facebook, Twitter and Instagram introducing new measures against conspiracy theorist hashtags, videos and content, removing David Icke's pages, banning QAnon apps and pages and deleting the 'plandemic' video, anti-Semitic material and Holocaust denialism. The anti-government marches risked more infections, whilst the Covid-19 misinformation and anti-vaccination propaganda led to increased hospitalisations and deaths. In the US, the Trump administration's anti-scientific administration ridiculed and undermined expert advice and promoted quack cures such as hydroxychloroquine and disinfectant, contributing to the death-rate. News stories began appearing about Covid-19 deniers who'd died, such as a 30-year-old in Texas who'd become infected at a 'Covid-19 party' (Pietsch, 2020).

This conspiracism regularly became violent. #Pizzagate had shown the danger of Alt-Right conspiracism (BBC, 2017b) and QAnon seemed to encourage violence, being implicated in the armed QAnon truck blockade of a bridge at the Hoover Dam in July 2018 (Mansell, 2020) and the October 2018 bomb parcels sent by a Trumpist to George Soros and Democrats (BBC, 2018). On 1st August 2019, the FBI identified QAnon as a domestic terror threat (Wilson, 2019). More attacks followed. In September 2019, there was an attack on a chapel for claimed involvement in child-trafficking; in April 2020, there was a derailing of a freight train in Los Angeles (United States Attorney Office, 2022); July 2020 saw the ramming of a truck through the gates of the Canadian prime minister's residence in Ottawa (Cecco, 2020); and November 2020 saw arrests for child kidnapping (BBC, 2021a). Coronavirus restrictions and anti-BLM marches saw the public appearance of armed pro-Trumpist, pro-conspiracy and QAnon-linked militia movements on the street, fuelling a danger that would find its realisation in the domestic terrorism of 6th

January 2021. Even after that, the threat continued. On 25th June 2021 a One American News (OAN) presenter publicly called for the 'execution' of thousands of 'traitors' responsible for the election 'coup' (Woodward, 2021).

Meanwhile, the Covid-19 pandemic mobilised right-wing militias, QAnons, libertarians, MAGAs and conspiracy theorists, leading, in the US and Europe, to violent anti-lockdown protests, physical assaults by people asked to wear a mask and the public abuse of journalists and scientists. 5G-related conspiracy theories led in the UK to vandalism and arson attacks on 5G installations and attacks on telecommunications workers (Hern,2020; Parveen & Waterson, 2020). In Wisconsin, a conspiracy-theorist pharmacist was arrested for sabotaging 500 doses of the Moderna vaccine as it could harm people and 'change their DNA' (Gorman & Spalding, 2021); in Italy two anti-vaxxers were arrested for an arson attack on a Covid-19 vaccine hub (Brenton, 2021); in the UK a fake bomb was sent to a vaccine production site in Wrexham (BBC, 2021b), whilst in Amsterdam a bomb exploded outside a coronavirus testing centre (Henley, 2021). Then, on 25th December 2020, Anthony Warner set off a huge vehicle-bomb in Nashville, US, targeting an AT&T hub, killing himself, damaging about 50 buildings and crippling cellular, internet and cable service across several states for two days. His motivation was online conspiracy theories, including the claim that shape-shifting lizards had infiltrated the government and were taking over the planet (Cavendish et al., 2021).

What we were seeing was a definitive change in the nature of terrorism. In the years leading up to Covid-19, Islamic State appeared to have perfected the use of the internet for terrorism, using their ability to publish instantly and globally to assault the world with their beheading videos, discovering singular acts of hyperviolent body horror could match the global-shock of 9/11 with less cost, organisation and risk (Merrin, 2018: 229). But this was still using the internet as the carrier of their message. In September 2020, Gilles de Kerchove, the EU counter-terrorism coordinator, suggested a 'major change in society' was underway, voicing his concern about the 'potential future rise of new forms of terrorism, rooted in conspiracy theories and technophobia' (Dearden, 2020). He was already too late. It was already here. Whereas both political and religious terrorism believe the existing system is the wrong one and must be transformed along the lines of their preferred earthly or transcendental ideals, conspiracy theorist violence is fundamentally different.

Here, the existing order is a con, a veil thrown over the hidden reality that only the select can see through; hence the aim of violence is the *exposure* of the real (of the personal reality of the conspiracist-terrorist). This is a new mode of *reality terrorism*, aiming not at the realignment of the real in accordance with an ideological or religious ideal, but the revelation of the already existing but hidden reality (Merrin, 2021). It takes aim at the officially produced and sanctioned reality principle, with the intention not of causing terror, but of alleviating it for the imprisoned, reality-washed population. This new era of terrorism, therefore, will be fought over reality itself, between those who live in different worlds. This *epistemological war* will be even harder to win than the 'War on Terror'.

It's easy to dismiss conspiracy theorists as cranks who have left the real behind, but this personal crafting of the real isn't as ridiculous as we might think. Walter Lippmann's 1922 book *Public Opinion* explained how individuals have always tried to make sense of their world, using media to help form pictures in their mind—'mental images', 'symbols' and 'fictions'—of the world beyond their experience, creating the reality they live within (Lippmann, 2007). As the world got more complex, Lippmann was critical of the ability of individuals to understand the world and, as a result, of their ability to participate in democracy. Hence his belief that the powerful broadcast media and the new arts of 'persuasion' could be benevolently used by an elite to direct and control their opinions—a process he described as 'the manufacture of consent'. The conspiracy theorists, of course, accuse the MSM of precisely this and it is true that the broadcast media were able to create a single, all-encompassing mass-consensual bubble, but, as we've argued, the digital revolution has blown this apart.

Digitality, therefore, constitutes a Ptolemaic revolution, reorienting media creation, distribution and consumption *around the self*, as I become the active creator and curator of my own reality. My central role today is as a *researcher of the real*: it is my job to explore and assemble the truths, facts, claims, opinions and arguments that explain the world to me and which I can live within. Hence conspiracy theory's promotion and celebration of the individual truth-seeker—the #pizzagate gunman's self-investigation, the QAnon exhortation to 'Do your research' and UK TV host Eammon Holmes's justification for questioning the media's rejection of 5G conspiracy theories as 'someone with an inquiring mind'

(Robinson & agency, 2020). Except, this is not simply conspiracy theorist activity: today it is the way each of us now relates to the world. As McLuhan suggests, we are 'hunter-gatherers' of information—as he presciently quipped, today, 'All the world's a sage' (McLuhan & Fiore, 1996: 14).

And this is why all attempts to combat 'fake news' and disinformation will fail. Apart from the arrogance of the very media that conspiracists distrust announcing they are doing the fact-checking for everyone, these attempts are all founded on the belief that if only people had the *correct* information, everything would be ok. But people don't lack information. It's not a problem of information *but of reality*: of the personalisation of the real and the connected foam-universes we create. Hence combating 'fake news' has nothing to do with media literacy or factual research: it is *an epistemological war*. Because, as Lippmann suggests, media technologies and their images have always been central to how we experience the world beyond our immediate experience. And as the media—these engines of reality—have been democratised to us all, so has their *world-making power*. Each of us harnesses and uses the power to make our own world.

Digitality, therefore, was our real pandemic: in unleashing the forces of *all of the people* ('pan'—all; 'demos'—the people), it left us both forced to and free to construct our own worlds and realities, liberating all of our personal experiences, thoughts, opinions, biases, inclinations and whims. The Covid-19 pandemic authoritarian countries like China suffered from their curbs on individual freedom of speech, dismissing discussion of Covid-19 as disruptive, anti-social rumours, but, when it was unleashed, they then benefitted from their ready ability to impose state controls on the population. In the west, in contrast, democratic governments were reluctant to impose restrictions (seeking to protect the market) and this, combined with a freedom to say absolutely anything—including denying the existence of the virus, attacking vaccinations and agitating to destroy our own communications infrastructure—impacted catastrophically on our ability to stop transmission. By December 2020, the US began a run of over 3000 Covid-19 deaths a day—equivalent to a daily 9/11 (McCarthy & Belam, 2020).

But the conspiracists aren't entirely to blame here. As Lippmann argues, we all need to find and collect information to make sense of our world. We are all doing our research into the real, but we are doing so now in a world of fractalised information. What conspiracy theorists are doing, therefore, is merely a parodic form of the 'research' we all have to do to make sense of the world. And conspiracy theorism is often built on tiny truths—the vaccine was developed very fast; there have been reactions to it by a minority; the question of the virus as being man-made (through 'gain of function' research) and a lab-leak still hasn't been resolved. In the age of hyporeality, when we need little or nothing to support our beliefs, that's enough to build our worlds upon.

Whereas Baconian empiricism built the *weight of evidence* from the sensory weight of the world and the weight of repeated observation, our hyporeality is built from our personal discoveries—our weightless, filtered and processed, templated photos, videos, comments, likes, stories and posts and the free-floating facts of our 'research'—of the truths, arguments, exceptions, anomalies, revelations and invented science we find. The hyporeal is a world without mass, weight or anything to hold it down. In the hyporeal, the hyperimaginary hyperinflates, floating free of the referential real of the terrestrial *body-of-evidence*, being given free rein in a parodic hyperfalsity where the self can declare anything as true and challenge any opposing real to dare to deny it, to give in to it and to admit its *deep truth*.

The pandemic should have had the opposite effect. The shared experience and risk should have rehabilitated the real: instead it exposed its explosion. This has often been interpreted as a rejection of experts—especially, of health experts—but it represents instead the explosion of experts. We were all forced to understand this new world and that's what we did, becoming experts in the new reality, clicksplaining the facts: what the virus was and how it worked, what the government was doing right, or wrong, what was happening in terms of treatment, drugs and vaccines, why it was and wasn't the same as the flu, why everyone else's interpretation of the lockdown guidance was wrong and what everyone should be doing, what facemasks could and couldn't do, what the risks of catching the virus outside or in a shop were, why social-distancing was essential, why 2 m was or wasn't enough, what the police had a right to do or not do, why there was a difference between the law and the guidelines, why it was a hoax, or an attempt to control us, or caused by 5G, why the media coverage was wrong or right, why we were all in it together and why we weren't, why this was and wasn't an attempt at forced vaccination, why the lockdown needed to end, or continue, and why another preferred country had a better way to deal with the virus. And all it was assembled from our 'research' and 'self-investigations'.

Everyone, not just the conspiracists, was doing the same, and everyone insisted that they were right. In the age of hyporeality, of personalised reality, your expertise and understanding always *trump* others. There have been many discussions in recent years of the 'crisis' of democracy, much of it wanting to blame social media. From a broader perspective, we can see that digital technology does indeed have a role to play here. Democracy depends on a shared world we all have to live within and on listening to other's opinions and compromising. The digital revolution has unleashed personal realities and individualised experience, forced upon us a much more complex process of sense-making and hyper-inflating our own voice and our own opinions, all of which we try to force back upon the world.

So we naturally look for others we agree with. We connect our personal bubble to others and form our foam worlds, entire communities taking from and giving to each other, with their foam rising and falling in unison. Because the word 'conspiracy' comes from the Latin 'conspirare' which means 'to breathe together' (hence its application to those who plot together and thus breathe the same air). Today, therefore, *we all conspire*: we all co-respire and we all create our co-respiratory theories of the world. With the explosion of our own personalised realities and the connected foam of our bubble universes, we are all simultaneously conspiracists and co-respiracists.

## The Victory of the Incumbent

The focus on conspiracy theorists as fundamentally different and deluded, therefore, obscures the way in which they are actually precisely like us. What, to us, seems to be people trapped in an unreality is better understood in terms of the explosion of mass-consensual reality. Contrary to the Democrat's never-Trumpism and Kamala Harris' late-campaign rhetoric warning of Trump's fascism and threat to democracy, for millions of Americans, *in their realities*, it was precisely that 'democracy' was the problem and Trump that was the solution. Indeed, for many, given the 2020 'steal', *Trump was actually the president* and this was merely the re-election of the incumbent. Hence he could campaign as simultaneously the real sitting president and as an outsider who would have run the country better.

This sharding of reality has been happening for nearly two decades now, since the take-off of broadband and Wi-Fi, the explosion of 'Web 2.0' platforms and the success of the smartphone from 2007, but we've been slow to recognise it, let alone understand its implications. The Democrats' post-election confusion highlights this. They thought they were reasonable, sane, safe, progressive, in favour of people's rights, defenders of democratic institutions and processes and careful overseers of a post-pandemic recovery and growing economy.

It turns out they were living in their own reality.

# CHAPTER 3

# The *Pornographic Obscenity* of Trump

**Abstract** Trump's 2024 victory was not a simple case of right-wing resurgence, but a result of a much broader and deeper public rage against a system they perceive as corrupt, indifferent and rigged against them. This chapter explores how Trump's appeal stems from his unfiltered, even pornographic self-exposure, which allows him to articulate the rage and frustrations felt by many voters alienated by established political systems. We explore the historical roots of representative democracy's inherent limitations, and that populism, exemplified by Trump, arises as a response to this systemic failure of representation. Whereas, traditionally, such exposure would destroy a candidate, Trump's political appeal was based precisely upon his own, personal *hyper-exposure*. As a celebrity politician, Trump's defeat will only come when his celebrity becomes too much, too boring. Whilst ever he articulates the public rage—and entertains the public with its expression—that won't happen.

**Keywords** Pornography · Rage · Mugshot · Scowl · Jean Baudrillard · Anti-political · Populism · Front stage · Back stage

In 1986, Jean Baudrillard published his travelogue book, *America*, recording the experiences of this quintessentially-European thinker of

W. Merrin and A. Hoskins, *SHARDED MEDIA*, https://doi.org/10.1007/978-3-031-84786-8_3

the New World. What he saw were the vast deserts, the deep geological time of Monument Valley, the LA freeways, the ecstatic circulation of cars, goods, signs and images, Hollywood cinema studios, the New York streets, the endless, empty, perpetual-motion of joggers and 'the exhilaration of obscenity, the obscenity of obviousness of power, the power of simulation' (Baudrillard, 1988: 27). And, above all this, as the ultimate symbol of 80s US, there was 'Reagan's smile'.

Americans love to smile, Baudrillard says, though not out of courtesy but instead from a seeming 'need to smile'. It is a smile that keeps you at a distance, a part of 'the general cryogenisation of emotions', like the smile of the dead man in his funeral home: for Baudrillard 'it is the smile of advertising' (1988: 33–34):

> It is also Reagan's smile – the culmination of the self-satisfaction of the entire American nation – which is on its way to becoming the sole principle of government. An autoprophetic smile, like all signs in advertising. Smile and others will smile back. Smile to show how transparent, how candid you are. Smile if you have nothing to say. Most of all, do not hide the fact that you have nothing to say nor your total indifference to others. Let this emptiness, this profound indifference shine out spontaneously in your smile. *Give* your emptiness and indifference to others, light up your face with the zero degree of joy and pleasure, smile, smile, smile ... And it works. With this smile Reagan obtains a much wider consensus than any that could be achieved by a Kennedy with mere reason or political intelligence. (1988: 34)

Reagan's entire credibility, Baudrillard concludes, 'is exactly equal to his transparency and the nullity of his smile' (1988: 34). As Jan-Werner Müller reminds us, Reagan was not always so smooth. As Governor of California, he was a proto-populist, early culture warrior, opposing the Civil Rights Act and Voting rights Act, 'seething with resentment' and spouting far-right anti-liberal rhetoric (Müller, 2024). By the time of his presidency, however, Reagan had transformed himself into an avuncular, media friendly statesman. Reagan's smile ruled the 1980s. Against this, today, we can contrast *Trump's scowl*.

## TRUMP'S SCOWL

Donald Trump isn't known for his smile, though it does manifest occasionally. When it does, it's the smile of egoism, self-certainty, smugness and self-congratulation, basking in his acclaim, in his bon mots hitting and in the enthusiasm of his crowds. Or it's the smile that accompanies the 'thumbs-up' whilst posing at the graves of soldiers killed during the 2021 withdrawal from Afghanistan (Kilander, 2024). In fact, when we think of Trump, we think of the opposite of Reagan's advertising-image friendliness. We mainly think of *Trump's scowl*. With his scowl, Trump achieves a consensus that no mainstream, smiling US politician could produce today.

A Google image search of Trump leads to a wall of these scowls, but there is one in particular that has become iconic. On 24th August 2023, after Fulham County, Georgia, indicted Trump on charges of election racketeering and issued an arrest warrant, Trump turned himself in at the Fulham County Jail in Atlanta, was booked, given the inmate number P01135809 and released on bond. Soon after, a photo of his mugshot leaked. Trump posted it onto X with the comment, 'MUG SHOT - AUGUST 24, 2023, ELECTION INTERFERENCE, NEVER SURRENDER!' and a fund-raising link for the 2024 campaign. As the first booking shot of a president in US history, this should have been career killing. It was to have the opposite effect. Trump would lean into the image and all that it represented, redefining in the process the entire concept of 'conviction politics'. In his pride in the indictment, he would demonstrate *the courage of his convictions*.

The image is off-centre, as if no-one, not even the law, could quite pin him down, make him obey, hold him under its disciplinary gaze. It's a clash of colours: the classic blue suit, white shirt, red tie, the trademark, huge blonde quiff and the orange of the face, reddened now with fury. Trump leans forward, as it to challenge us, as if he's about to hit us. His face is down, his jaw is locked in a grim, repressed expression and the eyes burn into us. It's a boxer's pose, the stance of a political pugilist. The image was embraced by his supporters, with the Trump campaign producing mugs, t-shirts and bumper stickers of it. In December 2023, Trump released the image as part of 'The Mugshot Edition' of his non-fungible token digital trading cards. 100,000 cards were initially released for $99 each, with options to get limited edition physical trading cards hand-signed by Trump and containing a piece of the suit he wore for the mugshot and an invitation to dine with him at Mar-a-Lago (Roush, 2023).

For his supporters, the mugshot was the perfect symbol of Trump's persecution. In *their realities*, this was a president who had won the 2020 election and had it stolen from him and now he was being persecuted for trying to 'stop the steal'. This was a political assault on Trump by his Democrat opponents and the deep state of the legal and political system, just as the over 600 people imprisoned for terms ranging from a few days to 22 years were all political prisoners. Days before the election, the Department of Justice continued to prosecute January 6th insurrectionists despite Trump's promise to pardon his supporters (Reilly, 2024). His mugshot epitomised this defiance of the law and his belligerence at due process and the values of democracy.

The mugshot was quickly recognised as one of the defining political photos of the era, but there might be another to challenge it. On 13th July 2024, Trump narrowly survived an assassination attempt at a rally at Butler Pennsylvania. The secret service bundled him to the ground then tried to move him. As they did so the Associated Press photographer Evan Vucci captured a defiant and bloodied Trump, raising his fist and shouting 'fight, fight, fight' to the crowd beneath a beautiful blue sky, perfectly—and unbelievably—framed by the US flag. And there it was again, the hard-jawed *Trump scowl*. Again, Trump immediately saw the financial opportunities, making the image the cover of a new book of photographs (Tait, 2024).

Trump's scowl. It's the preferred self-image of a man for whom his masculinity, testosterone, vitality and physical potency are so important to him. It's the projection of the political 'strong-man', of a real man who can get things done; it's not the image of discussion, debate or compromise, or of political astuteness, insight or wisdom. It's a scowl of fury, *of rage*. Because rage is the defining emotion of Trumpism, whether simmering away underneath the political surface, or exploding out in his outbursts or those of the insurrectionists. Trump's supporters feel that rage and see Trump's scowl as a form of direct political representation. His anger is theirs too. They love how he expresses what they think, what they *feel*, and, crucially, what you're not usually allowed to say. In contrast to Reagan's smile, with its empty and insincere incarnation of absolute US power, Trump's scowl is full and authentic: it's full of rage, full of meaning, and it threatens at all times to break out *against* the existing US system of power. This is Trump's populist, *anti-political* threat.

## THE *ANTI-POLITICAL* PARTICLE

Perhaps we shouldn't have been as surprised by Trump's return. The post-2008 crash has seen an increasing populist turn within and against liberal democracies. In the UK, it was heralded by the rise of UKIP and far-right groups such as the English Defence League and Britain First, becoming mainstream with the June 2016 Brexit vote, Labour's turn to Corbyn's left-populism from 2015 to 2020 and the success of Boris Johnson in 2019. In the US, it was marked by the first Trump presidency, and it's been seen across Europe with a series of far-right populist parties building their base and challenging for local, national and European elections. What Trump's re-election is signalling is that this isn't a blip, but rather a sign of a more fundamental problem with democracy.

The reason for this is because what we understand as democracy was, from the beginning, designed *against* the public. As A.C. Grayling points out, 'For many centuries the idea of democracy was regarded with revulsion and fear' (2018: 113). Plato's critique in *The Republic* that democracy represented a mob-rule—the rule of those not qualified or fit to govern (Plato 1988: 377)—was the dominant perception for centuries. As such, Grayling suggests, modern representative democracy was specifically designed to solve this problem of the dangers of actual public participation (2018: 113).

For Grayling, it was the 1647 English Civil War 'Putney Debates' that would revitalise the dream of a public democracy. Though these radical, participatory ideas would be quickly stamped out, the English Parliament would prove to be the origin of modern representative democracy. As Edward S. Morgan argues in *Inventing the People. The Rise of Popular Sovereignty in England and America*, the seventeenth-century English Parliament, looking for a legitimising basis to oppose a monarchy supported by 'the divine right of Kings' (1989: 17–37), increasingly found it in their role as 'representers' (1989: 23). Thus they opposed the 'fiction' of monarchical provenance with their own fiction: 'the sovereignty of the people' (1989: 36–37). This 'people' was formed not so much by the local constituents, but rather by the abstract idea of the entire realm; of a public that were 'far too numerous a group to deliberate or act as a body' and hence were represented instead by the parliamentarians (1989: 49). Popular sovereignty, therefore, was always a mode of simulation: it was 'an instrument by which the representatives raised themselves to a maximum distance above the particular set of people who chose them', endowing themselves with the abstract power of the whole (1989: 49–50). It excluded the real people, to preserve the government of the few.

This exclusion of the people from their own democracy was hard wired into the emerging Western liberal-democratic political structures. The US Constitution may have begun with the words 'We the people...', but only one branch of government, the House of Representatives, was popularly elected. The president was voted in by the state representatives of the Electoral College, the judiciary was unelected, with the Supreme Court justices being appointed, and the Senate wasn't popularly elected until 1913 (Grayling, 2018: 81–83). The UK has a similar structure with, again, only the House of Commons being voted for by the people. The Prime Minister is the ruling party's leader, being voted for by party members; the judiciary is appointed, whilst the House of Lords is partly inherited and partly appointed. All these systems were designed to symbolically (and practically) exclude the people. As Morgan concludes, 'representation has always been a fiction designed to secure popular consent to a governing aristocracy' (1989: 286).

Democracy, therefore, was representative democracy, but it's important to understand how this worked. MPs were not delegates, under the sway of their constituents and obliged to reflect their opinions. Instead, an aristocratic model prevailed: MPs represented their constituents by being the *best* of humanity—by their existence as worthy, superior beings, and by dint of their moral and personal qualities, their intelligence and their *breeding*. Hence Edmund Burke's famous 1774 'Speech to the Electors of Bristol', where he firmly stated that whatever else he sacrificed for his constituents, his 'unbiased opinion, mature judgment and conscience' he ought not to sacrifice for anyone, arguing, 'Your representative owes you, not his industry only, but his judgment; and he betrays, instead of serving you, if he sacrifices it to your opinion' (Grayling, 2018: 155).

Eventually the social, demographic, economic and political pressures of urban, industrial modernity led to significant electoral reform in the West. In the UK, a series of Representation of the People acts in the nineteenth century expanded suffrage, leading to the 1918 and 1928 acts that finally recognised and enfranchised modern, mass society. With these acts, modern democracy was realised and secured, but it remained a representative system. Over the following decades democracy in the North America and Europe made inroads into the 'hearts and minds' of its publics, especially with the 1930s New Deal in the US that did more than offer a remedy to the ravages of the Great Depression but also formed a model of expanded, benevolent and progressive government that would mark out a consensual politics for decades. The post-war settlement in the UK offered the same deal, ushering in 'the golden age of capitalism', with Fordist full-employment, high wages, a mixed economy of private and public, strong unions working with the employers, a strong welfare state, including education, health and a social security safety-net, progressive taxation limiting economic inequalities, improving living standards and easy to get consumer goods, and the opportunity of meritocratic personal progress, and a 'one-nation' politics with reduced political division and parties succeeding each other as managers of the same system.

The failure of this system, by the early 1970s, led to a search for alternative political solutions through the decade and the turn in the US with Reagan and in Europe, with Thatcher and Kohl, towards a new, right-wing neo-liberalism. This would transform the state and the world system over the following decades. Skip forwards and we find that, by the early millennium, and especially after the 2008 financial crash, many felt this political system was failing to represent them. Parties were becoming disconnected from their older roots and voters were becoming more volatile. The polished, suited, focus-grouped, PR-vetted, media-savvy, professional politicians trained to answer on air with bland, generic, non-committed answers had become the default. Career politicians with no experience beyond the world of university and party politics replaced those who'd grown in and through local jobs and institutions. Organised lobbying powers and financial donations dominated the political system, squeezing out constituent and elector concerns. Politicians became media celebrities, mixing with the world of entertainment, and political reporting seemed to form its own bubble, centred in the cities, reinforcing the idea of a 'metropolitan' elite disconnected and protected from the real, from the post-2008 job losses, debt and austerity.

Political events fed this discontent. The shock of 9/11, the 'War on Terror', the Bush and Blair government's cynical manipulation of evidence to promote the Iraq invasion, the drip-feed of deaths and the chaos of the Afghan and Iraq 'forever wars', and the 2013 Snowden revelations about Western governments spying on their own public all undermined the reputation of authorities. In the UK, the newspaper 'hacking scandal' and revelations of Jimmy Savile's abuse at the BBC turned many against the mainstream media, whilst the 2009 MP's expenses scandal exposed for many the venality of the political class at a time of financial hardship. Ultimately, as we'll see, it was the ravages of globalised neo-liberalism—de-industrialisation, the impact on jobs, cuts to welfare and services, the free movement of people, the migration problems caused by the global economy, wars and climate change and the turn to neo-liberal 'austerity' as its own solution to its own problems—that broke the spirit of many.

Meanwhile, a resurgent Russia and expansive China, the global threat of Islamic State after 2014, the civil wars in Libya and Syria, the nuclear ambitions of North Korea, wars in Crimea, eastern Ukraine and Gaza, and climate change-related disasters presented us with an increasingly chaotic and worrying world. Even in Europe, there was a rejection of the gains of pluralistic, multicultural liberal democracy and increasing complaints on the populist right and among conspiracy theorists of the power of 'global elites' and their machinations against the native populations. (For a discussion of these political problems of liberal democracy see Baldwin, 2018; Deneen, 2018; Guilluy, 2019; Kristev & Holmes, 2019; Levitsky & Ziblat, 2018; Luce, 2017, Mounk, 2018; Runciman, 2018).

This was the real political cause of Brexit and of Trump. The social contract of liberal democracy—*the simulated representation of representative democracy* in which the chosen at least claimed to (and sometimes actually *did*) operate in your name and in your interests—had failed. These were fundamentally protest votes against the system of representative democracy for that failure. The 'sovereignty' and 'control' the UK 'Leave' voters demanded in 2016 wasn't really aimed at Europe (which served merely as a symbol of its loss: in reality few in the UK could even name the key institutions of the EU, or their function). It was aimed, as much as anything, at the UK Parliament itself, demanding that it listens to and actually serves the people of the country. In the same way, the Trump voters in 2016 and 2024 rejected the Democrat's claim that 'democracy' was threatened by a Trump presidency. The Democrats simply didn't understand that the threat the voters felt was from *that existing system itself*. It was, again, a demand for politics to listen and to serve. Representative democracy, however, has a problem. It has proven resistant to change and slow even to understand the scale, depth and validity of the popular discontent. If the system is unable to change—and unlikely to be able to incorporate the radical participatory elements it has always avoided and fought to control—then, as Plato warned, the only path left is towards some demagogic figure. This is the populist revolt.

The subject of populism has given rise in recent years to considerable commentary (see especially, Eatwell & Goodwin, 2018; Judis, 2016; Mudde, 2017; Müller, 2017). Here, we would simply argue that populism is the public's solution to the problem of representative democracy: to a system that has broken even the promise of representation. Denied any external solution or reform of representative democracy, the public find one *internal* to the system, responding to a broken mode of representation with a *hyperrepresentation*. This is the turn to Plato's 'single popular leader' (1988: 386) who they launch like a missile into the system to act, not as another 'representative', but as a virulent hyperrepresentative: as a self-proclaimed, direct embodiment of the people. Hence the appeal of the populist as 'one of us', as a man or woman (regardless of the incongruity of their personal wealth) 'of the people', and the populist's projection of their own sentiments and desires as co-substantial with the people's. As Müller says, they 'provide a sense of direct connection with the "substance" of the people and, even better, with every single individual' (2017: 34). The populist, therefore, both acts within the democratic system by voting for a leader *and against it* in launching into it a free, radical, lone, anti-democratic, *anti-political particle*, who promises to sort it out, to cut through the red tape and bureaucracy, to push its rules, to break its inertia and restore to the people what they deserve and need.

The populist hyperrepresentative, therefore, radicalises the key democratic principle, the representation of the people, against the system, by acting as the simulacral realisation of direct, public participatory democracy. They appear as the *reality* of all the people, incarnated in one figure, in one body; a figure injected directly into the unhealthy system; into a system that doesn't want all of the people and that was built to keep them out and control them. And the populist radicalises too the basis of democratic legitimacy, 'the consent of the governed', to present it here as a direct mandate, *a will* fully embodied in their own, that allows them to act against the system itself from within, as it's what the people 'want'. As Müller explains, populists do not, of course, really represent all of the people; they usually intentionally represent only a part, demonising others who are denied national or political validity (Müller, 2017: 20–22), but as a simulacral representation of the people they can operate within democracy as a live, dangerous, unpredictable and toxic force; one containing the seeds, as Plato realised, of democracy's degeneration into 'tyranny' (1988: 382).

The elected populist anti-political particle is usually a centripetal force, in wanting to bypass constitutions, laws, precedents and rules, and accumulate power to themselves, to reward their in-group and rule according to their personal desires. Ironically, however, the effect of their centripetal power-grab is a decentralising and centrifugal effect on a polity they regard as the 'enemy within' (Stracqualursi, 2024). This is government by chaotic 'charismatic' personality; but not the stable, traditional charisma Max Weber analysed. Instead, it is a depthless, changeable self, based on a shifting play of signs, ideas, whims, off-the-cuff comments, personal obsessions and seat-of-the-pants, stream-of-consciousness; the whole held together by their ego. The populist personality, therefore—think Boris Johnson and Trump—is fundamentally *ex-centric*, in the dual sense of their characteristic oddball-personality and in their exertion of a destabilising, centrifugal force against the rules, processes and ways of governance of the political centre.

It is no coincidence that Johnson's Britain and Trump's US were two of the nations that fared worst in the 2020 Covid-19 pandemic. Both prioritised personal liberty and economic freedom and resisted the full mobilisation of the centripetal powers of a state they ideologically opposed. Both *ex-centric personalities* refused to take advice or accept expert opinions: they were suspicious of medical expertise and scientific advice, personally reckless about their own susceptibility (and subsequently caught the virus), delayed or opposed lockdowns or government intervention leading to increased death rates (a total of 232,112 deaths in the UK and 1,219,487 deaths in the US), were reluctant to engage state power in response and preferred, where possible, to promote free-market business. Often, they tried to wing it by sheer force of personality, using their whims, populist *bon homie* and jocular ad-libs to deal with both critics and complexity.

Trump, especially, became a global spectacle. He blamed China for the 'Kung Flu' (BBC, 2020b), declared the virus would evaporate in the April heat (Levin, 2020), claimed on the day of the first death that the virus would 'disappear' one day, 'like a miracle' (T. McCarthy, 2020), later said the virus was a 'hoax', rejected state requests for central government help and advocated his own solution of trying the anti-malarial drug hydroxychloroquine, saying 'It may work, it may not work … I feel good about it. It's just a feeling … What the hell do you have to lose?' (Smith, 2020a). He'd later suggest injecting disinfectant would be 'a great thing to look at' (BBC, 2020a). As late as 29th October 2020, on a day when 1004

US deaths were recorded, he mocked expert advice about mask wearing (BBC, 2020c). US deaths would hit a one-day height of 5463 on 12th February 2021.

## TRUMPIAN *PORNOGRAPHY*

The real scandal of Trump isn't that he won the presidency, it's the fact that he could run, carry out his campaign and win—*all in public*. And do it twice.

Liberal democracies have long been built upon a separation of the 'public sphere' and the 'private sphere'. The private sphere is the realm of the home and family and the space of retreat from the vicissitudes and labour of the everyday public realm. It was the Victorians who perfected and—typically overly-sentimentally—valorised this space (Merrin, 2005) which would become the political obverse of the public sphere (see Habermas, 1989). Hence, whereas one was responsible for everything one said and did in public, especially as an elected official or candidate, the private sphere was where one could relax and express candid thoughts among family and friends. Unless there was a leak, the worst aspects of one's personality could find free rein, without the pressure to conform to all acceptable public opinions. Within modern political journalism, the private life, therefore, became fair game: any muck about hypocrisy, immorality or illegality in the private life of a public figure was newspaper cat-nip, certain to ruin a political career. This was justified by the self-congratulatory, 'whig' theory of the press: that its aim was to hold those in public office to account, to expose the wrong doings of the powerful to aid democracy. Transparency, therefore, was the perceived route to democratic accountability.

The problem is this no longer applies, as Trump cannot be exposed in the traditional sense as his entire politics is based on *an auto-indemnified self-exposure*. When Trump tweets about the delicate, sensitive issue of negotiating arms control with the North Korean leader Kim Jong-Un—'I told Rex Tillerson, our wonderful Secretary of State, that he is wasting his time trying to negotiate with Little Rocket Man…' (BBC, 2017c)—the entire diplomatic world catches its breath over the outrageous presidential comment and risk to world peace. To no effect. Trump is indemnified by his own troll-politics, by his chaotic love of the lulz, by his playing with reality, his offensiveness and love of mockery, and, above all, his own pornographic obscenity.

For a theory of pornography, we return to Jean Baudrillard in his 1979 book, *Seduction*. As we saw in the last chapter, Baudrillard's discussion of pornography is closely linked to his theory of the production of the real. Western, semiotic media societies don't just produce the real, they devote themselves obsessively to this production and to its 'hyper-reality'—to the forced materialisation of the real in all its hi-fidelity, high-definition, technologically-realised exactitude. This, he says, is a mode of pornography. As he says (quite beautifully) about pornography's desperate attempt to represent sex: 'The only phantasy in pornography, if there is one, is not a phantasy of sex, but of the real, and its absorption into something other than the real, the hyperreal' (1990b: 29). Hence, the attempt to semio-technically realise the absolute truth and reality of sex is a project that says more about our relationship to reality itself and to our project of forcing it into existence: 'Modern reality no longer implies the imaginary, it engages more reference, more truth, more exactitude, - it consists into having everything pass into the absolute evidence of the real' (1990b: 29). Baudrillard's example is the Japanese 'vaginal cyclorama', where men pay to push their faces as close of possible to the genitals of presented sex-workers. As Baudrillard says, 'in order to see better – but what?'. Everything pales, he says, 'before this moment of absolute obscenity, this moment of visual voracity that goes far beyond sexual possession' (199b: 31–32).

What is really exposed here, therefore, is not the genitals, or even sex itself, but rather a desire to make everything available *in its absolute truth and reality*. This is the Western desire especially to realise the real:

> ... what is involved is an *orgy of realism*, an *orgy of production*. A rage ... to summon everything before the jurisdiction of signs. Let everything be rendered in the light of the sign, in the light of visible energy. Let all speech be liberated and proclaim desire. We are revelling in this liberalization which, in fact, simply marks the growing progress of obscenity. (1990b: 32)

This is a culture, Baudrillard says, of the desublimation of appearances: 'a pornographic culture par excellence; one that pursues the workings of the real at all times and in all places' (1990b: 34).

This is the realm of the 'obscene', of the materialised, hyper-visible rendition of the real, of an 'over-representation' that is so perfectly, technologically realised, open and beyond refusal that, as in the Maussian gift and symbolic relationship, 'you have nothing to add, that is to say, nothing to give in exchange' (1990b: 30). One simply *burns* from the absolute, open transparency, the forced production of the real. Trump, therefore, represents this obscenity. He cannot be exposed by traditional politics or journalism as *he is already pornographic*. His entire politics is based on *self-over-exposure*: there is nothing held back here.

Consider his 2016 election campaign:

At a rally in South Carolina he mocked a disabled *New York Times* reporter, Serge F. Kovaleski, who suffers from arthrogryposis, a condition that affects the movement of joints, going so far as to mimic his body spasms and contorted arm (BBC, 2015).

In December 2015, he said climate change was merely 'weather', said the nation should institute 'a total and complete shutdown of Muslims entering the United States', praised Vladimir Putin, said that when Hilary Clinton lost to Obama she'd got 'schlonged', boasted about calling everyone 'stupid' ('I went to an Ivy League school. I'm very highly educated. I know words, I have the best words…') (Mashable, 2016).

In October 2016, it emerged that he boasted, on a leaked tape (from 2005), how, as a 'star', he could grab any woman 'by the pussy' and 'do anything' to them (Fahrenthold, 2016; Martin et al., 2016), he accused Hilary Clinton of having 'hate in her heart' and later threatened her with criminal prosecution if he became president, he repeated claims the election was 'rigged', he body-shamed Hilary's sexual attractiveness ('… when she walked in front of me, believe me, I wasn't impressed'), he criticised the sexual attractiveness of a woman who'd accused him of sexual misconduct, and he suggested Hilary needed a drug test before another debate (Mashable, 2016). (See Mashable, 2016, for an astonishing timeline of further examples.)

*Nothing* affected him. What should have killed any other campaign only seemed to strengthen Trump. He gained 62.9 m votes and 304 Electoral College votes and became the 45th President of the US.

The 2024 election campaign was no different, being marked by Trump's fury, abuse and racism. In 2023, he called 'radical left thugs… vermin', described immigrants as 'poisoning the blood of our country', claimed he would be the 'retribution' for conservatives, suggested Mark Milley, then chair of the joint chiefs of staff deserved 'death' for having previously tried to constrain his presidency, threatened lawyers for the federal special counsel Jack Smith that he was 'coming after' them, threatened to indict his enemies after re-election, called Alvin Bragg, the

Manhattan district attorney, 'a Soros-backed animal' and the writer E Jean Caroll, 'a whack-job', and admitted that, during his presidency and after, he'd 'been waging an all-out war on American democracy' (Pengelly, 2023). During a November 2024 Milwaukee rally in Wisconsin Trump experienced technical difficulties with a microphone. His response was to simulate oral sex, gagging over the microphone (Lubin, 2024). He was re-elected with an increased popular vote of 74.6 m votes and 312 Electoral College votes, becoming the 47th President of the US.

Erving Goffman published his classic, *The Presentation of Self in Everyday Life*, in 1959 (Goffman, 2022). He describes here a 'dramaturgical approach' to the self, famously dividing our relationship to the world in terms of a 'back stage' and a 'front stage', like the theatre. In the front stage, the actor engages in 'impression management', controlling the communication of self to remain consonant with the assumed public role, in contrast to the back stage where one can be oneself. Trump breaks this dichotomy. *Trump has no back stage.* He can't help himself. Everything passing into his mind passes immediately into the front stage in *a perfect post-modernist stream of lack-of-consciousness.*

In October 2019, after a female astronaut corrected him during a video call to the International Space Station, he was seen to instantly, reflexively, put his hand to his head and give her the finger (Christian, 2019). The same month Jimmy Kimmel mashed together a clip of Obama's dignified, presidential announcement of the killing of bin Laden, with Trump's announcement of the death of Abu Bakr al-Baghdadi (Michallon, 2019). Whereas Obama announced that 'the United States launched a targeted operation against that compound', Trump said, 'they did a lot of shooting, and they did a lot of blasting, even not going through the front door. You know, you would think you go through the door. If you're a normal person, you say, "Knock, knock. May I come in?"'. Whereas Obama reported, 'After a firefight, they killed Osama bin Laden and took custody of his body', Trump says of al-Baghdadi, 'He died like a dog', which prompted the comment, 'Our K-9, as they call — I call it a dog, a beautiful dog, a talented dog — was injured and brought back'. Trump ends with 'And I'm writing a book. I think I wrote 12 books. All did very well'. Everything comes back to him and whatever he was thinking in the moment.

A series of insider tell all books appeared during Trump's first term, revealing the story of the presidency. In January 2018, the internet fell victim to a Twitter parody appearing to come from Michael Wolff's new book, *Fire and Fury* (Wolff, 2018), which claimed that Trump, in his first day in office, had complained that White House televisions did not carry 'the gorilla channel' and that Trump then spent hours a day watching gorilla programming his staff subsequently had to produce to satisfy his love of gorillas. So many people believed it that the Twitter user had to clarify that 'the gorilla channel thing is a joke' (Nelson, 2018). Other books seemed like a parody but weren't. These included *A Warning* by 'Anonymous – A senior Trump administration official' (Anonymous, 2019) which described Trump as 'like a 12-year-old in an air traffic control tower, pushing the buttons of government indiscriminately, indifferent to the planes skidding across the runway and the flights frantically diverting away from the airport'. His Twitter antics left his advisors, 'in a full-blown panic', Anonymous says, before adding:

> It's like showing up at the nursing home at daybreak to find your elderly uncle running pantsless across the courtyard and cursing loudly about the cafeteria food, as worried attendants tried to catch him ... You're stunned, amused, and embarrassed all at the same time. Only your uncle probably wouldn't do it every single day, his words aren't broadcast to the public, and he doesn't have to lead the US government once he puts his pants on. (Koran, 2019)

Whereas, traditionally, such exposure would destroy a candidate, none of this impacted upon Trump. This is because his political appeal was based precisely upon his own, personal *hyper-exposure*.

Everything about Trump was obscene. What he articulated was three-fold. First, he said what wasn't being said by Republican politicians, about the 'deep state', 'the swamp', the mainstream, legacy, lying 'fake news' media and the elite political class. Second, he said what couldn't be said because of 'political correctness', including all the anger at Hilary's feminism, the disabled, black people, homosexuality and LGBT. Third, and most importantly, his transparent, fully-open, obscenity meant he could say *what his voters really wanted to say*, letting it all out. Because as we all know, you can't say anything these days; even jokes are banished. You can get 'cancelled' for anything, and Trump let them express it by proxy. He let it all hang-out.

In 1964, the Frankfurt School Marxist, Marcuse, published his classic work, *One Dimensional Man*. In it, he argued that the processes of 'desublimation'—the expression and exploration of pleasures—were now 'repressive', in binding humanity to a capitalist society offering 'false needs' that substituted this pleasure for revolutionary change (Marcuse 1991). Today we can reverse that and offer up a new psycho-political element that definitively protects and defends the existing capitalist reality: that of *desublimated repression*. Desublimated repression is the pleasure of unburdening oneself, of being able to say '*fuck political correctness*' and admit to the transparent, obscene rage against the other—against race, sexuality, gender and all of that—and promote a demand for the public repression of identities, classes and all categories of the human you want to deny. Desublimated repression is the ironic, 'joking' (but totally serious), public admission of the love of Fascist exterminationism, with all the lulz of violent hatred and the dream of its realisation. It is what Trumpism is and lets you be.

Trump, therefore, is the symbol and epitome of *desublimated repression*: of the anti-political-correctness dream of uncontrollable offensiveness; of letting-it-all-out; of a *neuro-divergent Fascism* we keep having to deny exists. Trump is the open, obscene, transparent force of racism, misogyny, hatred and anti-democracy, hyperrealised in front of our eyes, and we still daren't quite fully call it out. How then can Trump fail? We can't expose him, as that exposure is the source of his power. Perhaps Putin has 'Kompromat' that would bring him down (Ray, 2021). But realistically, for his supporters, that would only expose the international or deep state attempt to bring him down. Plus, is there anything Putin might expose that could ever harm a figure we have seen everything from already? As a celebrity politician, Trump's defeat will only come when his celebrity becomes too much, too boring. Whilst ever he articulates the public *rage*—and entertains the public with its expression—that won't happen.

# CHAPTER 4

# The *Rage* of the People

**Abstract** The rage at liberal democracy—at the seeming disinterest of contemporary representative democracy to take an interest in the public and support them—we set out here as also a product of the economic devastation wrought by global neo-liberalism. This anger, shared by both the working class and the super-rich, was effectively harnessed by the populist right, who targeted liberal-progressivism's emphasis on identity politics and the perceived failures of globalisation. The resulting nativist backlash focused on immigration, multiculturalism and foreign intervention, scapegoating these issues as symptoms of a deeper malaise. We conclude that ultimately this rage is a direct consequence of decades of neo-liberal policies that have created highly-unequal societies, leaving the majority feeling abandoned and powerless.

**Keywords** Culture wars · Identity politics · Neo-liberalism · Politics of rage · Racism · Misogyny · Democracy

When the scale of Donald Trump's victory on 5th November 2024 became apparent, the Democratic Party's panicked post-mortem began. There were no shortages of candidates for the blame, with anger focusing on Biden running again or leaving it too late to stand down; the failure to run primaries for a new candidate; Harris's lack of policies; her lack

W. Merrin and A. Hoskins, *SHARDED MEDIA*, https://doi.org/10.1007/978-3-031-84786-8_4

of engagement outside of mainstream media; her campaign focus on abortion, transgender issues and on Trump's 'fascism' and threat to democracy; the Democrat's lack of appeal to the young; the problem of disinformation and right-wing propaganda; their lack of focus on economic issues; Harris's association with the incumbent presidency and its problems; the over-use of celebrity endorsements; the loss of assumed Democrat voters, especially among the Latino and Black community; Harris's attempted appeal to the right or to a vanishing centre; or perhaps Harris's failure to be left-wing enough and appeal to the working class, or even that she was too left wing (see Adragna, 2024; BBC, 2024b, 2024c; Epstein et al., 2024; Goldmacher et al., 2024; Hubler, 2024; Pengelly, 2024; Volpe, 2024).

All these are valid discussion points, but the more important and uncomfortable question is not why did Harris lose but why did Trump win? Knowing now what he was, and seeing him openly campaign on authoritarian threats, how did he appeal to so many and, indeed, do so well, sweeping the swing states, winning the popular vote and helping the Republicans take both the House and Senate? To understand this, we need to understand how Trump's scowl and personal fury succeeded as the direct reflection of a rage felt by his supporters. This is a widespread rage today, seen in Europe too, for example in the 2024 success of the UK Reform Party, the French National Rally party, the German AfD and the illiberal parties of Eastern Europe as well as in South America. It is a rage taking many forms—from the simmering discontent expressed in angry social media posts and online comments, through to outbreaks of violence, such as the US 6th January 2020 insurrection and the summer 2024 UK riots.

Given its electoral expression, one obvious interpretation is that this is a rage felt by 'right-wing' and 'far-right' supporters, but these categories risk simplifying a more complex phenomenon which has a broader basis. Rather, it is more accurate to say that it is the populist right that has best succeeded in capturing, reflecting, amplifying and focusing the otherwise broad, incoherent, emotional rage of the electorate, unifying this disparate public in the process around a simple set of issues, explored below. In the process, it has also achieved a remarkable coalition of those who have fared worst in global neo-liberalism with those who have benefitted the most. Because, ironically, this is also the rage of the super-rich, whose anger is also directed at liberal democracy, for (as we'll see) their own reasons. Together this combined popular and elite anger has unleashed and promoted to prominence *a politics of rage*. Their key, shared grievance is with liberalism and its cultural, political and economic systems.

In the last chapter, we saw the public's widespread political disconnection from and distrust of contemporary representative democracy—of liberal-democratic government systems and their institutions, laws, rules and procedures. Many people now believed that even the pretence of representing them and their interests had disappeared. For them, government had been captured, whether by professional politicians, by the complicit MSM, by a 'metropolitan' or 'cosmopolitan' elite, by the 'deep state' officials, civil service and public servants, by new 'global elites' and by the power of major financial lobbyists, super-rich donors, global companies and 'big pharma'. The exact nature of that capture and the groups in control varied according to your view of the system and the extent of your personal 'research' and immersion in alternative media, but what's important is that, however ridiculous the fringe conspiracy theories are, many people appear to hold broadly-similar sentiments about the system and its operation.

There was an old joke about how it wasn't worth voting as the government always got in; a joke usually told with a jaded wink and a what-can-you-do? cynicism. Now, however, it was less a joke than a shared, deep-seated anger at the system. In this increasingly held view, liberal democracies had become enclosed, self-serving systems geared towards the few: towards a circulating elite whose role had simply become the technocratic management of *the simulation of democracy* and the promotion of the state as *a global neo-liberal actor* for their own benefit (whether whilst in power, or, after, in the lucrative consultancy market, the media and invited-speaker circuits, or the Davos lunches).

It is this political crisis of representative democracy together with the economic crises caused at a national level by neo-liberal policies that form the background to the rage of Trumpism and the populist right. Two days before the US election, Ezra Klein argued that this wasn't a battle between the left and right, or even between the Democrats and Republicans as traditionally understood, but instead it was a battle around 'the basic worth of institutions': as to whether or not you still believed in these governmental systems or not. Whilst the Democrats had faith that these systems were doing their best and remained trustworthy, in contrast:

The Trumpist coalition sees something quite different: an archipelago of interconnected strongholds of leftist power that stretch from the government to the universities to the media and, increasingly, big business and even the military. This network is sometimes called the Cathedral and sometimes called the Regime; Trump refers to part of it as the Deep State, Vivek Ramaswamy calls the corporate side 'Woke Inc.' and JD Vance has described it as a grave threat to democracy. (Klein, 2024)

In this sense, Klein concludes, Trump's campaign and electoral coalition isn't conservative, 'it's counterrevolutionary'.

Despite, however, the framing of much of the right-wing discourse within Trumpism and the European far-right as *against the left*—as fighting, when the spittle really gets flying, 'Marxism', 'Cultural Marxism', and even 'Communism'—this is largely untrue as the left holds no real power or influence in the west today. In reality, the targets of the right owe far more to liberalism as a political, economic and cultural philosophy, hence the power of their attacks on contemporary liberal systems. The three targets of the populist right today—what they're really taking aim at—are not left-wing. Instead it's liberal-progressivism, global neo-liberalism and liberal democracy.

## The Rage Against Liberal-Progressivism

By anti-liberal-progressivism, we mean the 'culture wars'. Essentially, this is a public opposition to what is seen as the overreach of identitarianism, or 'identity politics', encompassing especially issues around sex, gender, sexuality and race. One partial explanation of Harris' defeat is the obvious expression of racism and misogyny at a black, female candidate, but beyond that there was also a broader hostility to a party and its younger, progressive, activist base, seen as leaning harder into identity politics than voters were comfortable with (despite the fact that Harris' campaign showed few signs of campaigning on those issues).

Trump exploited this. After the September 2023 debate, his campaign pushed a TV ad attacking Harris for her obscure 2019 commitment to fund surgeries for transgender inmates and her pledge that 'every transgender inmate in the system would have access'. The ad's tag-line—'Kamala is for they/them. President Trump is for you'—worked so well they put more money in to repeat it (Goldmacher et al., 2024). Trump's concomitant commitment to impose wide-ranging restrictions and roll-back civil rights protections for transgender students such as Title IX protections highlights the importance of this issue for his campaign. Again, we can see an obvious prejudice here, but also the ongoing impact of the QAnon conspiracy theory. Though its hysterical claims about paedophile elites had faded after his 2020 defeat, the ideas subsequently metastasised and were filtered through mainstream Republican politics, finding expression in the wave of book bans around LGBT+ books and opposition to 'Drag Queen reading events' (Gabbatt, 2023; Petri, 2023). The common theme of these attacks, in claims of 'grooming' and overly-sexual interest in children, highlights the continuing influence of the QAnon moral panic. The Summer 2023 US public boycott of Bud Light beer due to its link-up with the transgender influencer Dylan Mulvaney shows how deep that issue had become for many (BBC, 2023).

The hypermasculinity of the Trump campaign can also be seen as an opposition to identitarianism, this time targeting women. Trump had been worried about the issue of abortion, though in the end his success with white women suggests this wasn't a defining issue for them. Recognising the voter importance of younger men (including black and Hispanic men) alienated by perceived left-wing ideology, his campaign leaned hard into bro-culture misogyny, with Trump linking himself to the Ultimate Fighting Championship, getting Hulk Hogan to speak at his rallies and associating with online male influencers such as Joe Rogan, with his three-hour podcast with Rogan getting 45 m views on YouTube (Goldmacher et al., 2024). Resurfaced remarks from his vice-presidential candidate J.D. Vance in which he called Democratic women 'a bunch of childless cat ladies with miserable lives' also emphasised the latent misogyny of his campaign (Looker, 2024a).

Race also remained a continuing issue for the Republicans and the right in America. In the aftermath of the George Floyd #BlackLives-Matter protests, there was a political backlash from Republicans at a new bogeyman they blamed for fomenting racial hostility: Critical Race Theory (CRT). By 2021, a number of states had introduced legislation to ban the discussion, training and/or orientation in schools that the US was inherently racist as well as any discussions about conscious or uncon-scious bias, privilege, discrimination and oppression (Ray & Gibbons, 2021). Universities became part of this racial, identitarian battleground for Republicans, with the Supreme Court overturning affirmative action in admissions in June 2023 (Debusmann Jr., 2023) and with the emergence in 2023–2024 of opposition to University DEI (Diversity, Equity and Inclusion) policies (Lawrence, 2024). The late 2023–2024 attempts to clamp down on pro-Palestinian speech on campuses fits into the broader political problem of race, though here identitarians were also often seeking to protect Jewish groups from hate speech (Binkley, 2024).

Trump's camp tried to exploit race, with Trump claiming Kamala Harris had emphasised her Asian-American heritage until recently when, he claimed, 'she became a black person'. 'I didn't know she was black until a number of years ago when she happened to turn black and now she wants to be known as black', he told the National Association of Black Journalists in Chicago in June 2024 (Looker, 2024b). Hours after Trump's victory, many black people reported receiving racist texts telling them they'd 'been selected to pick cotton at the nearest plantation', with instructions for how to prepare (Walker, 2024).

It's not hard, therefore, to find overt prejudice at work here, but it's successful because it taps into a broader and politically-profitable opposition to 'left' identitarianism. The 'culture wars' work because they engage strong emotions and become framed in terms of existential status threats to the opposing identities. In a world in which the 'privileges' of the dominant identities have been significantly eroded politically and economically (see below), a 'left-wing' emphasis on the need to upend these privileges even further, and, indeed, ever more radically, is experienced as a significant threat and, indeed, the final straw. But this threat is also strangely empowering. Because although those suffering from it can do little about the problems caused by a global neo-liberalism and the international financial system, or about the unrepresentativeness of their democratic systems, they *can* do something about the culture wars, fighting back vocally and online against the madness of 'political correctness'. Hence the cultural centrality of these 'wars'.

Ironically, although we associate this identity politics around sex, gender, race and sexuality now with the left, contemporary identitarianism is better understood as an extension of liberal political philosophy. It's worth tracing this history to see how its current expression fits in.

It was John Locke, in his 1689 book *Two Treatises of Government*, who put forward the classic liberal argument that men are created equal by God ('Men being, as has been said, by Nature, all free, equal and independent') and that they possess certain 'natural rights' including the right to life, liberty and the enjoyment of one's property. As the 'state of nature' they live within is a realm of pure freedom, allowing anyone to threaten one's rights, then people come together, Locke says, to form a 'compact', agreeing to give up rights against each other that are then invested in 'one body Politick' whose role is to protect these rights. Full individual rights for all, therefore, lie at the heart of liberal political philosophy (Locke, 1965: Sections 95–99). Though this was presented as an abstract, universal philosophy, it wasn't. Locke was writing in defence of the 'Whig' aristocracy, defending their rights not to be killed, imprisoned or to have their lands seized by the crown, hence the roots of liberalism were a class-based revolt against the monarchy. The mid-seventeenth-century Civil Wars, then the 1688 Glorious Revolution and 1689 Bill of Rights represented its final success, in forcing the monarchy to submit to aristocratic parliamentary sovereignty.

The Lockean ideal was quickly transposed to the US where a successful revolution against English rule led to the 'Declaration of Independence': the founding document of the US, announcing the separation of the 13 North American British colonies on 4th July 1776. The declaration's second paragraph is already familiar, stating, 'We hold these truths to be self-evident, that all men are created equal, that they are endowed by their Creator with certain unalienable Rights, that among these are Life, Liberty and the pursuit of Happiness' and claiming that to protect these rights governments are formed from 'the consent of the governed' (National Archive, 2024). In reality, however, 'all men' didn't mean all men, with black people and Native Americans especially being exempt from this ideal. Even after the abolition of slavery, with the passage of the 13th amendment in 1865, it would take until well into the twentieth century before the political rights of women, black people and Native Americans were accepted.

The same fight for rights had to happen in eighteenth-century Europe too. The 'radical' tradition of liberalism agitated for equality, with Thomas Paine arguing for the 'rights of man'—meaning now all men—in 1791 (Paine, 1985) and Mary Wollstonecraft famously adding the rights of women to this in 1792 (Wollstonecraft, 2004). Slavery was gradually abolished in the British Empire by the Slave Trade Act 1807 and the Slavery Abolition Act of 1833, whilst the same period saw Socialist and Marxist Communist agitation for the rights of the working classes (Marx & Engels, 2004). The middle classes won their own political recognition with the 1832 Reform Act, but it would take until the aftermath of

World War I before the voting rights of the working class and women were granted across Europe.

This gradual European recognition of rights wasn't extended around the world. In the late nineteenth century, European nations embarked on a frenzied, capitalist colonial expansion through Africa and Asia that was justified by a newly-virulent racism, denigrating the bodies, minds, humanity and existence of the colonised and leading to rampant atrocities and even genocide (Lindqvist, 1996). The liberal ideal of 'all men' being equal wasn't honoured here. That projected racism would later be internalised back into Europe, finding its fullest expression in Nazism— as Lindqvist argues: 'Auschwitz was the modern industrial application of a policy of extermination on which European world domination had long since rested' (1996: 160). Post-war de-colonisation, therefore, was aimed not only at ridding nations of colonial powers but also, as Frantz Fanon understood, of a colonial mindset that denigrated the humanity and individual rights of the colonised (Fanon, 2021).

Modern, Western identity politics connects to these traditions, emerging in the US from the mid-1960s, with the 'Second Wave' of Feminism, after the publication of Betty Friedan's *The Feminine Mystique* in 1963 (Friedan, 2010); with new racial movements such as the Civil Rights movement and the emergence of 'black consciousness', 'black pride' and 'black liberation'; and with the 'gay liberation' movement, which followed the NYC Stonewall Inn riots from 28th June 1969. These movements had an ambiguous relationship to the left. Though inspired in part by the post-war anti-colonial 'liberation' movements which followed Marxist and Maoist ideas—applying these now back onto those internally-colonised by the west—they were also aimed *against* the Western New Left and radical politics whose emphasis on class, capitalism and working-class organisation overlooked or ignored issues such as sex, race and sexuality. (Feminists, for example, tired of being asked to make tea for their comrades and have sex for the revolution.) The identity politics that emerged through the 1970s, therefore, ultimately owed more to liberalism, as the radical extension and realisation of its doctrine of equal, individual rights.

With the failure of the political left in the 1970s in the US and Europe, with the turn to the right following the 1973 global depression, there were only two options left for radicals by the early 1980s: either move to the centre, to rebrand as a kinder manager of the now-dominant neo-liberalism (the strategy that would eventually work for Bill Clinton and Tony Blair), or identity politics. The latter sucked up many radicals, convinced they were the leading-edge of radical left-wing politics, whereas, in truth, they represented the abandonment of the economic, class-based analysis of capitalism in favour of a theory of natural rights and their final realisation for excluded minorities. As identity politics developed through the 1980s–90s, it was still possible to find theoretical elements of the left (in, for example, the influence of Gramsci, the Frankfurt School and Structuralism), but there was a far greater influence from continental literary theory: from post-structuralist theories of power, discourse and binary oppositions and from post-modernism's attack on normative metanarratives and the construction of the real. Importantly, these were all movements that, at the time, the left virulently opposed, condemning the work of thinkers such as Derrida, Foucault and Baudrillard (Callinicos, 1989; Kellner, 1989; Kellner & Best, 1991; Norris, 1990, 1992). In the 1990s, these strands of liberal political theory, post-68 continental theory and an individualistic (neo-liberal influenced) therapy culture would merge on the campuses into modern identity politics. Overall, the left played a smaller part in this than is usually supposed. Ideas of 'political correctness', no-platforming and cancellation may have had roots in left politics and fitted into liberal identity political strategies, but on the whole the left represented an economistic analysis that the latter had left behind.

Hence contemporary identity politics rests upon a syncretic and often contradictory theory. Much of it actually takes aim at 'liberalism'—whether in the post-modern critique of its metanarrative, the post-structuralist deconstruction of the liberal self as a product of discourse, the radical Feminist movement's attack on patriarchal culture or Critical Race Theory's structuralist attack on white privilege and the links between liberalism and white supremacism. However, in practice, this is countered by the *felt belief* of identitarians that their identity really exists as a simple, core, natural and real *inner truth* that requires practical action to promote and defend. Hence, despite the theory itself, liberalism's ideals of equality and natural rights remain at the core of the movement's politics and of the personal expression and rights-based aims of its adherents.

The modern antipathy to 'identity politics', therefore, isn't really an opposition to the left, to the 'Woke', to Marxists or Communists. This is all a straw-man, as the radical left is weaker than ever before, having little real political force or power today. Instead, it's a fundamentally prejudiced opposition to the liberal idea that we are all, indeed, created equal and deserving of the same rights and treatment. The reason this has become so popular is due to the second and most important target of the populist right: global neo-liberalism.

## The Rage Against Neo-Liberalism

The contemporary crises of representative democracy and of liberal-progressivism are intimately linked with, and are an explicit reaction to, the national crises caused by the era of economic, global neo-liberalism. The late 1970s' 'neo-liberal' economic turn, inaugurated by Margaret Thatcher in the UK and Ronald Reagan in the US, swept away the remaining social-statist legacies and provision of the twentieth century: the US New Deal ideal of government projects and aid for the poor and working class, the war-time economies of state control and the post-war Fordist, Keynesian social-welfarism that provided for everyone 'from the cradle to the grave'. In the UK, it deliberately broke up the state in order to reduce its ownership of industry (and privatise national assets) and to reduce the welfare state provision that took up tax-payer's money, inflated wages and distorted the market. Cutting state spending, privatisation, the promotion of share-holding and tax-cuts were core neo-liberal principles. Another was the deregulation of markets and finance, as part of a drive towards the perfected globalisation of capitalist trade. Policies here included the deregulation of interest rates, the removal of credit controls, the privatisation of government-owned banks and financial institutions, the growth of investment banking and the globalisation of financial trading (see Steger, 2017: 38–61).

Global neo-liberalism was marked, therefore, by a de-industrialisation of the west, the emergence of a massively-expanded, cheaper, non-unionised global labour force in developing countries (such as China and India), globalised economies and deregulated markets and finance, the revolution of trade caused by information technology and containerisation, and the imposition of the 'Washington Consensus' upon developing nations, using the World Bank, International Monetary Fund (IMF) and World Trade Organisation (WTO) to force them to conform to the US neo-liberal model. From now on, national governments had little control over this global market or their own currencies (Steger, 2017: 66). As Streeck argues, the result was a 'hyperglobalisation'—an abdication or expulsion of nation states from their position as masters of their domestic and external economies, 'in favour of a "free play" of global "market forces"' (Streeck, 2024: 25). Just as the post-war governments were reduced to 'one-nation' managers of Keynesian economies, so, now, parties of the left and right were reduced to functionaries of the global neo-liberal market.

The crisis of Fordist accumulation in the 1970s also led to related 'Post-Fordist' changes in industry and business. Now 'flexibility' was the mantra, in the production process, in labour relations and in the market, etc. Innovation was emphasised, along with the use of new IT to allow smaller, faster, more mobile responses to the de-massified market. New digital technologies allowed greater coordination of the production, distribution and retail process, with 'just-in-time' production, stock-holding and service and automation where possible. This led to changes in the labour market within the west, where a small core of permanent, full-time workers would be complemented by a periphery of non-unionised, often part-time, temporary or agency workers, who could be more easily laid-off, had fewer worker benefits (holidays, sick-pay, insurance) and fewer rights (see Harvey, 2000).

In the UK, the impact of Thatcher's neo-liberal revolution (1979–1990) was a reduction in state-income and hence the slashing of spending on social provision, the destruction of traditional industries (in order to neuter the union movement), increased unemployment, reduced welfare provision, the devastation of communities and of entire geographic regions (the North and South Wales), the move to a service and information economy workforce, and a significant increase in poverty and inequality. After her fall in November 1990 (and that of John Major's Conservative neo-liberal government in 1997), from 1997 to 2010, Tony Blair's 'New Labour' attempted to provide a popular 'Third Way' between welfare-Keynesianism and neo-liberalism. In effect, however, it offered little more than an ameliorated neo-liberalism, with the government attempting to nationally manage and reduce the worst aspects of the global system. It was neo-liberalism with a minor, apologetic and desultory redistribution, by a party worried about scaring the markets.

By the early millennium, the effects in the UK of this decades-long neo-liberal revolution were pronounced, with fewer traditional and life-time jobs, an expanded service sector (swapping miners and steel-workers for baristas and call-centre workers), stagnant and low wages, the rise of 'precariat', 'zero-hour' and 'gig-economy' contracts and a public consumerism based upon cheap, globally-produced goods and credit-card debt (Standing, 2016). Social mobility had been reduced; education no longer guaranteed improvement (and, indeed, saddled many with life-long debts); the benefits system was hardened against the poor, with a complex web of 'sanctions' for infringement; 'food banks' were common; 'in-work poverty' was widespread; the NHS and mental health provision was broken, and, unless they could inherit wealth, new generations had fewer opportunities for stable, salaried work, housing and children than their parents. Those who were poor, unemployed, or of poor physical and mental health suffered most. The working class, especially in the 'left-behind' areas, also bore the brunt, whilst the middle classes felt their daily survivability slip away, splitting off between a small minority, who became more successful in this economically-polarised world, and the majority, whose lives now looked indistinguishable from the struggling working class. Meanwhile, 'the 1%' were doing fine (Dorling, 2015).

By 2008, 'the increasing volatility of financial flows combined with three decades of neo-liberal deregulation to produce a global meltdown' (Steger, 2017: 46). Though the financial crash was caused by neo-liberal economic policies (by the deregulated banking sector and its high-risk lending practices), in the UK the outgoing Labour government's public spending got the blame, leading to a decade of conservative 'austerity' from 2010, promoting hard-line neo-liberalism as the solution to neo-liberalism's own global failure, slashing state provision and spending even further. Meanwhile, the 2015 Panama Papers exposed how the global rich avoided tax and social responsibilities (ICIJ, 2024); news stories exposed massive tax-avoidance by the big tech companies, and there was an increasing discussion of the '1%' and the globally-cosmopolitan 'super-rich' who had prospered from this massive wealth-transfer.

In December 2020, a study by David Hope and Julian Limberg confirmed what was obvious about neo-liberalism: that 50 years of tax-cuts (from 1965 to 2015) had helped only one group—the rich. The economic theory went that tax-cuts would spur and aid individualistic entrepreneurialism, leading to profitable businesses, increased employment opportunities and a resulting 'trickle-down' of wealth throughout society. The authors found that per capita gross domestic product and unemployment rates were nearly identical after five years in countries that slashed taxes on the rich and in those that didn't. But the one major change was that incomes of the rich grew much faster in countries where tax rates were lowered. Tax cuts for the rich led not to a trickle-down of wealth, but rather aided the rich in keeping more of their wealth, exacerbating income inequality (Picchi, 2020). Indeed, the analysis supports instead the policies of the post-war era: as Hope and Limberg suggest, 'if we look back into history, the period with the highest taxes on the rich — the post-war period — was also a period with high economic growth and low unemployment'.

The US underwent a similar neo-liberal revolution, following the tax-cuts, reduced state spending, deregulation and global free-trade policies of Reagan, Bush and Clinton through the 1980s–90s. This was felt, most famously in the 'Rust Belt', a geographic region spanning SE Wisconsin, Illinois, Indiana, Michigan, Ohio, Pennsylvania and parts of New York State. Formerly 'the Steel Belt', this was the industrial heartland of the US from the late nineteenth century, through the twentieth century (peaking in the 1950s–60s), with its core industries focused on auto-mobile and steel production, coal-mining and raw materials processing. This region suffered especially with the post-1973 movement to neo-liberalism. As McQuarrie argues, high labour costs and strong unions meant de-industrialisation began with the movement of firms to the South of the US, where laws were more hostile to unions, before the region was hit by Japanese competition for its car industry, German and Japanese competition for its steel and an energy shift away from coal towards oil and natural gas (McQuarrie, 2016). The Clinton years in particular (1993–2001) were marked by the Democratic Party's aban-donment of its working-class base in favour of free-trade agreements allowing foreign competition, tax breaks for firms moving jobs overseas and tax preferences for financial rather than industrial investment, all of which would devastate the region. For them, the result of Clinton's neo-liberal, global-trade agenda was wage-stagnation and reductions, attacks on unions (whose membership plummeted in the following years) and, ultimately, plant-closures and redundancies (McQuarrie, 2016).

Political attempts to emphasise home-ownership and investment to maintain standards of living backfired, with the loss of pension and retire-ment savings in the tech bubble and of homes in the foreclosure crisis. The Democratic Party nevertheless continued with its neo-liberal poli-cies. As McQuarrie says, in response to the 2008 crash Obama 'chose to bail out bondholders while leaving homeowners to rot' and then pursued more free-trade policies, 'expanding the number of countries that Amer-ican workers would have to compete with' (McQuarrie, 2016). Economic decline brought falling tax revenues, urban decay with rusting factories and abandoned houses, a declining infrastructure and population loss. Disinvestment and unemployment were compounded by drug addiction.

The loss of male jobs especially meant more emphasis was placed in the family on women's income, impacting on the crisis of identity felt by many former workers. As McQuarrie concludes, the Democratic Party had no interest in their problems: 'The Democratic coalition is a party of free trade, finance, and tech with a diverse base recruited on the basis of social liberalism and fluency with identity politics. This is not a party of the working class and is especially not a party of the white working class' (McQuarrie, 2016). The same analysis held true for 2024.

What we're seeing now, therefore, is a political backlash against global neo-liberalism due to its impact within national economies. You'd assume that it would be the left that would benefit from and best-mobilise resistance to this decades-long movement, but the opposite has been the case. Left-wing academic, political and economic critiques of neo-liberalism have had limited impact upon policy-makers whilst the working class one might have expected to be radicalised have lost their jobs, their unions, their communities, their civic institutions and their collective power. Small moments of hope for left-populism—in the urban Occupy movement (2011–2016) and the campaigns of Bernie Sanders in the US (2015–2016; 2019–2020) and Jeremy Corbyn in the UK (2015–2020)—clashed with more fundamentally-conservative and neo-liberal centre-left party authorities and failed to produce lasting mass-movements. In the UK, the right-wing press, as expected, excoriated Jeremy Corbyn's Labour leadership, but so too did Katherine Viner's centre-left *The Guardian*, which ran daily attacks on his leadership to destroy left-populism (LSE, 2016). Left-behind, lost, atomised and linked only by poverty, insecurity, resentment and polarised social media, with no major party offering anything more than a rootless, no-future, hyperglobalised more-of-the-same, all that was left was a quiet rage. Lacking any class-based connection or party expression, this rage became a free-floating particle, open to anyone who could capture and express it.

Hence, in the US, UK and Europe, this rage found its closest ally in populist, nativist, right-wing and even far-right parties and groups. It's easy to dismiss the result as inherently racist and even proto-Fascistic—as, indeed, its expression often is—but this *politics of rage* succeeds precisely because of its ability to draw a broader coalition of people together who all feel the same political disconnection and economic impact. Much of the social media flak produced from the right and far-right (MAGA or Reform, for example) takes explicit aim at what they see as fundamentally 'Wokeist', left-wing, Marxist or Communist targets that are apparently threatening Western civilisation, but, as in the 'culture wars', this is an ideological smokescreen, because what the populist, nativist right is really opposing is global neo-liberalism. Their primary targets—immigration, multiculturalism, foreign intervention (in aid or wars), the lack of protection of native workers, jobs and provision and the power of global elites and market forces—are all effects of, or represent, the post-1979 global neo-liberal revolution.

The most obvious target of the populist, nativist backlash is immigration. There is a clear racism here, in the right-wing hostility to 'foreigners', to claims of 'invasion' and conspiracy theories about the 'great replacement' of populations (Camus, 2018, 2024), but if we draw back from those modes of expression, we can see that the real target is globalism. There has been a significant expansion of immigration over our life-times. As recently as 1993, net migration in the UK was 1000 people, but from 1994 onwards we see a fluctuating, but gradually-increasing net migration, rising through to 2015 (a net of 329,000 people), falling by 2020 (93,000 people) and then spiking afterwards with a significant rise in numbers, with 484,000 people in 2021; 872,000 in 2022; and 866,000 in 2023 (Statista, 2024). Overall, in the forty years from 1950 to 1990, the UK population rose by 6.9 m (from 50.3 to 57.2 m), whilst it has risen by 6.9 m again in the last 16 years alone (2007, 61.3 m–2023, 68.2 m). Importantly, the post-war years were years of full-employment, growth and social provision, more able to integrate migrants, whereas the period since 2007 has been dominated by the 2008 crash, the subsequent recession and neo-liberal austerity, all of which made the economic and political issue of immigration more toxic.

Something similar has happened in the US. The US has always been a land formed by immigration, with the peak being from 1900 to 1914, when an average of 900,000 people arrived per year. This later stabilised, dropping to an average of 332,000 per year from 1961 to 1970 and 449,000 a year from 1971 to 1980, but subsequent decades saw a significant growth in numbers, with an average of 733,000 per year from 1981 to 1990, 909,000 from 1991 to 2000 and 1.04 m a year from 2001 to 2015 (EHA, 2024). In real terms, you can trace the increase in total immigration from 1.43 m entering in 1997, to 2.16 m in 2008, to a high of 2.70 m in 2016, with a slight (Covid-19-related) fall before the numbers rose again to 2.56 m in 2022 (USA Facts, 2024). 2023, the year before the election, saw an increase of another 1.6 m on 2022s figure, representing 'the largest single-year increase in the nation's immigrant population since 2000' (Gramlich & Passel, 2024). Overall, Leonhardt says, 'The immigration surge since 2021 has been the largest in U.S. history, surpassing even the levels of the late 1800s and early 1900s' (Leonhardt, 2024).

It doesn't matter whether native populations experience this migration or not, as the images of small boat crossings in the UK and immigrant lines on the southern border of the US produce the same feelings and responses. Immigration has become the core populist and nativist issue precisely because to local populations *it represents globalism*: it is the physical manifestation of the world, of its seemingly limitless population movements and of an unceasing threat to local jobs, housing, resources, government spending and defined cultures. Even legal migration is seen as a threat, in representing global population flows and the opening up of nations to the world. The EU's neo-liberal free-trade region demand for the free movement of peoples within its economic zone, for example, was one of the key factors behind the 2016 UK Brexit vote, with the fear especially of 77 m Turkish people being eligible to move turning many to vote no (BBC, 2016b). This nativist reaction isn't even interested in the positives of migration (in the provision, for example, of essential services such as the NHS): for them, there is only a desperate rage at and refusal of the outside world.

The common right-wing opposition to 'multiculturalism' in the UK represents another aspect of this anti-globalisation. This rejection of diversity was central to the reaction to the identification of the Southport attacker (whose killing of young girls sparked the Summer 2024 riots), as 'Cardiff-born Axel Muganwa Rudakubana' (Sandford et al., 2024). The far-right instantly rejected his Britishness, focusing on his Somali refugee family, his colour and his assumed Muslim faith: as one far-right Tik Tokker asked, 'If a rat is born in a stable, does that make it a horse?' In the ensuing riots, this concept of Britishness was solely white and Christian dominated. In Middlesbrough, rioters were even filmed stopping cars and screening the drivers for ethnicity, asking 'Are you white? Are you English?' (White, 2024).

TikTok was flooded with AI-generated pro-Reform and pro-riot images and videos, though there was a paucity of 'English' culture to represent, hence the reliance on cliched tourist images of London, Big Ben, London buses and taxis and union jacks. Images of Lions dominated too, along with the St. George's Cross and crusader knights. The iconography was frankly pathetic, but, again, underlying the racism was a desperate response to the external world and its changes. This was the desire of an economically-threatened and struggling population to turn the clocks back to the world of their childhood: to a world of white faces and communities, of a single wage-earner supporting their whole family, of less traffic on the roads, of real summers like 1976 and winters with snow, and only a few brown faces. Despite immigration long-preceding Thatcherism, the ideal 'imagined community' (B. Anderson, 2016) of today's nativist is instead *of the time that they knew*—of the 1960s–70s: precisely the time before the neo-liberal revolution; before the world and its cultures came to the UK and demanded resources and rights. The Britain they hanker for is a truly *Great* Britain, fixed in the unmemory of mediated-nostalgia; a Britain before de-industrialisation, globalisation, immigration, low wages, diversity, 'political correctness' and dinghies on beaches.

The populist turn against foreign intervention follows the same anti-globalist pattern. The era of the 'New World Order', when, following the revolutions of 1989 and fall of the USSR in 1991, America was a unipolar force able to project power and advocate for international democracy, brought little for those at home. The post-911 neo-con global 'War on Terror' led to 'forever wars' in Afghanistan and Iraq, thousands killed and wounded, vast amounts of money spent on the deployment of forces, private security, failed democracy-building and expensive infrastructure projects, the destabilisation of entire regions and a resulting increase in global migration flows, many heading to Europe, Germany, France and the UK. Over the next decade (2011–2021), the failure of Libyan intervention, the reluctance to intervene in the Syrian civil war, the global terror of Islamism and of Islamic State, the withdrawal from Iraq and the humiliating endgame in Afghanistan turned many in the US against the external world in favour of a renewed, 'USA-First' isolationism. Hence, Trump's isolationism in 2016 and his disinterest in Ukraine in 2024 reflected the feelings of many of his supporters. Similar sentiments could be found in the UK where the entire relationship of the nation to the world was being questioned, whether in continued anti-EU sentiment, Islamophobia, opposition to support for Ukraine and Reform supporters' continued attacks on foreign aid as wasted money. The populist reaction to global neo-liberalism and liberal interventionism rejected global links and global obligations: forget democracy abroad, where was *their democracy?*

Because, faced with governments oriented out towards the world—towards free-trade, global financial flows, global democracy, international diplomacy and relations, wars and foreign policy—the nativist reaction is the demand that *it* be the focus of concern; that *it be looked after*. If the Lockean origin-point of liberal government was to honour the social compact by protecting the rights of the citizens, then where had that protection gone? In truth, it was neo-liberalism that broke the post-war social welfare compact that they remembered: the compact that the state cared about you and would provide for you *in extremis*. Neo-liberalism's individualism, however, had made it clear you were on your own: as Margaret Thatcher famously said, 'there is no such thing as society' (Margaret Thatcher Foundation, 1987).

Now, after decades of this global neo-liberalism—of the stripping away and deterioration of state support and services and of globally-oriented economic and political policies—many had had enough. Their response, however, in targeting migrants, was an attack on the symptoms not the real cause. The overwhelming majority of the public were so far removed from the world of the tax-avoidant, globally-mobile super-rich that opposing them was pointless. Instead, the populist right was able to give a focus to and visible target for that rage, using simple ideas and powerful economic arguments. When it was reported that the cost of housing and supporting a single asylum seeker had risen in 2023–2024 to £41,000 a year (Bancroft, 2024), the maths for a working population with an average wage of £31,461 appeared simple: migrants got more than them, for free. The UK far-right's claim that this was money that should be spent on UK pensioners or veterans was deliberately emotive, but when there was a cost-of-living crisis, with rising food and energy costs and many in the UK relying on food banks, the underlying grievance wasn't without foundation.

The turn to housing immigrants in 'hotels' (with all the sense of luxury that implied) and even claims they would have access to 'private health care' (Cotterill & Tozer, 2024) provoked much online fury, finding real-world expression in protests outside hotels and, later, riots and arson attacks against them. The underlying rage, however, is really directed at a government spending money on others when its own people have been hit so hard by the global neo-liberal revolution and are struggling. Just as the UK Leave campaign weaponised the claimed £350 m a week paid to the EU as money that could be spent on the NHS (BBC, 2016a), so the UK's 2023 spend of £8.3 m *a day* on migrants became a powerful symbol of the government's perceived dereliction of its duty to its own people (Francis & Eardley, 2023). Again, a rage at the global system and neo-liberal government disinterest—its radical, deliberate desocialisation of care, support and communities; its cutting loose from all obligations to its own public; its excommunication of its population from a now-orbitalised, technocratic political system—found a hyperreactive expression in nativist populism.

It also found expression in conspiracy theorism. One of the most common of these is the idea that a 'global elite' or 'globalists' are really in control and deliberately driving the ruin of nation states and their populations. Once again, there's a racist expression here, as traditional anti-semitic tropes dominate in their identification of those who are in control and in claims about the ethnic 'replacement' of white, native populations. The list of those responsible, however, extends to include lizards and aliens, wealthy philanthropists (including Bill Gates and George Soros) and international organisations such as the World Economic Forum. The specific claims are extreme and comical, escalating in wildness as one immerses oneself in the alternative media, but, again, underlying them are some significant truths. Since the launch of the neo-liberal revolution, there *has* been a concerted effort by governments, transnational corporations and global financial institutions to push for the success of that single, integrated, global financial and economic system. The US *has* pushed the 'Washington Consensus' on developing nations through the power of the World Bank, IMF and WTO and 'global elites'—high-level politicians and super-rich business owners and oligarchs—*have* all attempted to increase the scope and success of this system for their own benefit. Underneath it all, conspiracists are right. The 'conspiracy' of 'global elites' working against the interests of those struggling in the global neo-liberal system they rage against is a real one: it's the *actual* conspiracy of normal, fully-functioning capitalism.

Rage at global neo-liberalism has occasionally broken through in a more explicit, direct form, at first in protests from the left, then, more recently, from the populist right. The 1988 anti-globalisation protests in West Berlin at the annual meetings of the International Monetary Fund and World Bank were one early example, as were the November–December 1999 Seattle World Trade Organisation demonstrations, which saw 40,000 activists protest globalisation and fight the police on the streets. The 2008 financial crash saw widespread anger at the bailout of banks with public money and the austerity politics pursued by many governments around the world. By October 2011, the Occupy movement had begun in the US, which inspired related demonstrations and linked anti-austerity protests worldwide. This left-wing critique of neo-liberalism would eventually fade, however, having had little political impact. They'd be replaced in the following years by more right-wing populist economic protests, such as the gilets-jaune (Yellow Vest) protests in France from November 2018, which also inspired international demonstrations in 2018–2019. With the pandemic, however, right-wing populist anti-globalism shifted to target instead national Covid-19 restrictions and government lockdowns (as seen in the Canadian and French convoy movements).

It may, however, have found a new expression in late 2024 after the New York City killing of the UnitedHealth healthcare insurance company CEO Brian Thompson on 4th December. When it was revealed the bullet casings had the words 'delay', 'deny' and 'depose' inscribed on them, most assumed it was someone angry at being denied insurance ('delay' and 'deny' being tactics used by insurance companies to avoid payout, whilst 'depose' means to remove from a high position). As Tufekci notes, the public response to the murder was marked, not by sympathy, but instead by a widespread hostility towards a business that epitomised, for many, the worst aspects of neo-liberal profiteering (Tufekci, 2024). Memes, jokes and celebratory comments went viral, going beyond the expected online provocation: as Tufekci says: 'The rage that people felt at the health insurance industry, and the elation that they expressed at seeing it injured, was widespread and organic'. On Facebook, for example, the announcement by the UnitedHealth Group that it was 'deeply saddened and shocked at the passing of our dear friend and colleague' was met, Tufekci notes with 80,000 reactions, with 75,000 of them being the 'haha' emoji (Tufekci, 2024).

Days after the murder a look-a-like competition was held in Washington Square Park, with the winner celebrating the gunman's actions (Meko, 2024). Soon after, Luigi Mangione (26) was arrested for the murder. He was found with a short note blaming the healthcare industry, saying 'Frankly, these parasites had it coming'. These insurance companies, he said, 'have simply gotten too powerful, and they continue to abuse our country for immense profit because the American public has allowed them to get away with it' (Klippenstein, 2024). There was an initial attempt by the right to cynically-frame Mangione as an anti-capitalist Marxist, but this received a strong push-back from ordinary people who offered support (Gabbatt, 2024). The sentiment wasn't new: a 2023 poll showed that nearly a quarter of Americans agreed with the claim 'American patriots may have to resort to violence in order to save the country' (Smith, 2023). As the rage against the health insurance industry shows, the possibility of this public anger supporting, promoting and turning to actual violence is very real.

## The Rage Against Liberal Democracy

The real cause of contemporary rage, therefore, is the effects of over four decades of globalised neo-liberalism upon the local economies of nation states which have transformed Western nations into highly-unequal, deso-cialised societies in which an elite prosper and the majority from the middle-class down, struggle with an increasingly precarious everyday life, impacting upon every level of their physical and mental health. The rage at these effects of globalisation find their simplest and most powerful expression, however, in a nativist populism that has been best captured by the right and far-right, giving rise to political expressions that are often racist, violent and destructive of liberal ideals of respect for the rights of all. Hence the rage expressed at liberal-progressivism and identity politics.

A key part of this liberal-progressive politics is the notion of 'privilege'—for example 'male privilege' or 'white privilege'. This concept infuriates the right in the UK and has led to legislative bans by Republicans in the US who refuse to acknowledge it. Yet the entire point of this privilege is that it's invisible and taken for granted. (A white male, for example, could walk through a space and not be stopped and searched by police, and hence not see that space as racialised, believing instead in its fundamental neutrality.) Those who have dominant, privileged identities, therefore, rarely notice that privilege, but what they *do* notice is the effects of decades of neo-liberalism: they notice what is missing, the loss or deterioration of services, the cost-of-living, the reduced opportunities, the unfairness of the system and their own plummeting wealth and social value. To be told *then*, by identitarian politics, by the mainstream media and company DEI policies that they *are* privileged and that their privilege needs to be ever more radically explored and challenged, is a politically-combustible situation. Hence the reaction against liberal-progressivism is really rooted in a deeper *loss of value* caused by global neo-liberalism. If nineteenth-century Western, industrialising economics was defined by 'surplus value'—by the profit extracted from the working population—then twenty-first-century Western, de-industrialised economics is defined by how much of that population is now *surplus to value*.

The rage at liberal democracy we explored in the last chapter—at the seeming disinterest of contemporary representative democracy to take an interest in the public and support them—is also, therefore, a product of global neo-liberalism. Because, for a long time, the state *did* take an interest. In the UK, in the nineteenth century, it curtailed the worst working practices of laisser-faire capitalism by introducing Factory Acts and union acts that stopped its extreme exploitation; in the early twentieth century, it introduced welfare legislation to mitigate the worst impacts of capitalism on the life of the worker, and, following the state control of the war-economy, it introduced a welfare-Keynesianism that, for decades, provided benefits, education and health for the population, taxed the rich for the good of all, boosted social mobility and owned key industries, ploughing the profits from essential services, back into the public purse. The dissociation from representative democracy, therefore, is intimately linked to the neo-liberal destruction of this state promise and service, the capture of politics by money, the professionalisation of politics, and the transformation of all politicians into the elite servants of neo-liberal, anti-social-statist orthodoxy.

The only response possible of an abandoned population, with no civic or social institutions to organise within, with no means of political transformation within the voting system, suffering from a pandemic of loneliness and dissociation (Corbin, 2024), and the simulated communication and community of digital technologies and with an algorithmic curation of content based on anger and engagement (Rose-Stockwell, 2023), *is rage*

Coincidentally, it is a rage also felt by the elite; by the very winners of global neo-liberalism.

# CHAPTER 5

# The *Rage* of The Elite

**Abstract** This chapter addresses the essential coalition—and contradiction—between the populist right and the Silicon Valley elite in supporting Donald Trump. This is the combination of the anti-progressive, anti-liberal-democratic, anti-globalist, nativist public, and the anti-progressive, anti-democratic, *but pro-global neo-liberal* economic elite. Whilst **the public** desired a return to domestic focus and state support, **the elite** aimed for a radical neo-liberal restructuring that minimised state intervention. This divergence stems from differing interpretations of 'disruption', with the public seeking re-engagement from the state and the elite pursuing an 'exit' strategy. We profile the key rageful players here, including Elon Musk and Peter Thiel, showcasing their ideological shifts and contributions to the 'broligarchy', namely which leverages technology and anti-democratic sentiments to further its goals. This chapter concludes by considering the potential for the fracturing of this coalition, and the prospects of this rage being turned back on Trump.

**Keywords** Broligarchy · Marc Andreessen · Elon Musk · Peter Thiel · Trumpianism · Philosophy of exit · People vs. the elite

It wasn't just the rage of the public that fed into the success of Trump, there was also the rage of the elite—of multimillionaires and multi-billionaires who also recognised in him a valuable anti-progressive and anti-democratic force. As the beneficiaries and supporters of global neo-liberalism, however, their motivations and hopes were actually the exact opposite of the public's. This is the essential coalition—and contradiction—that forms the electoral base of Trump's success: the combination of the anti-progressive, anti-liberal-democratic, anti-globalist, nativist public, and the anti-progressive, anti-democratic, *but pro-global neo-liberal* economic elite. Ironically, what Trump combined was precisely the losers of global neo-liberalism with the most successful winners of this movement. To an extent, this coalition is a direct reflection of the contradictions of Trump himself, in his nativist and neo-liberal incarnations. Although they have proven highly successful in forming a disruptive political force, the contradictions of this coalition still risk creating a schism in Trump's policies and administration from 2025. Because both poles, the public and the elite, voted for disruption, but, as we'll argue, *what* disruption they want and *what effects* they hope for are fundamentally different. To understand the rage of the elite, therefore, we need to understand this group, to recognise what they oppose and why Trump is seen as the solution to their problems.

## THE TRUMPIAN *BROLIGARCHY*

The internet and our digital life have undergone several phases of development. The first, from 1969 to 1994, was an era of creation, where the online, digital world was a new space—a separate world apart, devoid of authorities (Barlow, 1996; Davis, 1998), where those with the skills and ability to access it felt their way through this emerging 'world of mind', inventing their own selves, behaviours and communities (Rheingold, 1993; Turkle, 1996). The second phase, from 1995 to 2004, was a transitional era of mass discovery, when the World Wide Web took off, the broader public began to access the internet, commercial companies began to enter this realm and organisations and individuals began to have a web presence. From 2005, however, we entered the era of 'Web 2.0', a term coined by Tim O'Reilly to describe the movement from a web that was largely read-only to one where new private 'platforms' created 'rich user experiences' and new 'architectures of participation', hosting personal profiles and user-generated content (UGC) (O'Reilly,

2005). With the spread of home broadband and Wi-Fi, and user-friendly, internet-enabled smartphones (with the iPhone in 2007), a new world of social media, UGC, blogging and micro-blogging blossomed, through sites such as WordPress (2003), MySpace (2003) Facebook (2004), Flickr (2004), YouTube (2005), Reddit (2005) and Twitter (2006).

This new world in which everyone could produce, collaborate, share and organise gave rise to a wave of optimistic commentary, lauding the new technologies and their pro-transparency, pro-democratic and critical potential—indeed, even their radical democratic potential, as they didn't simply represent the public but constituted a new mode of real, collective participation, transforming older, top-down political, economic and cultural structures (see Anderson C., 2006; Benkler, 2006; Gillmor, 2004; Jenkins, 2006; Leadbetter, 2008; Shirky, 2008). Real-world, global events seemed to bear this out, with social media organised and inspired pro-democratic 'revolutions' in Ukraine in 2004 and Moldova in 2009, the 2009 Iranian election protests and the early successes of the 'Arab Spring' in Tunisia in 2010–2011 and Egypt in 2011. Democracy, it was believed, was spreading over the world, challenging authoritarianism, in a re-run of 1989.

US companies were at the heart of these events and, at first, the US government crowed about the new US-led globally-democratic forces (Clinton, 2010, 2011). Silicon Valley itself seemed happy to identify with these movements and these historical developments. Though their underlying philosophy had earlier been described as the pro-libertarian, techno-optimistic, neo-liberal 'Californian ideology' by Barbrook and Cameron (Barbrook & Cameron, 1995), the Web 2.0 era was explicitly characterised by a more socially-invested liberalism, seeing technology as supporting not only democracy, but positive social and communal values and social justice. In their outward comments and actions and internal company policies early tech-bros such as Mark Zuckerberg, Jeff Bezos, Elon Musk and Marc Andreessen were liberal, socially concerned and philanthropic, explicitly hoping to improve the world. And they often swung towards the Democratic Party.

By 2013, however, there was a growing criticism of this optimism and a recognition of the negative and anti-democratic effects of digital technology (see Keen, 2007; Goldsmith & Wu, 2006; Zittrain, 2008; Lanier, 2010; Turkle, 2011; Morozov, 2011; Pariser, 2011; MacKinnon, 2012; Deibert, 2013). Real-world developments also brought political disillusionment as the Western intervention in Libya failed, Egypt experienced a military coup and the Syrian pro-democracy movement met harsh repression, leading to a complex civil war and the ascendency of Islamist opposition. Meanwhile, Putin, from 2012 in Russia, and Xi Jinping from 2013 in China began to develop their own, closed 'sovereign' internets, using the same digital technology lauded as pro-democratic to identify and clamp down on political opposition. Then Islamic State from 2014 showed what uses Web 2.0 could be put to, to virally spread its terror (Merrin, 2018: 218–244).

By 2016, we reach the era of backlash. By then, the internet had birthed the 'alt-right', letting loose far-right ideologies that aided the election of Trump, and had incubated the UK Brexit vote. The subsequent post-presidential election revelation of the exploitation of social media by Russian disinformation and Cambridge Analytica's targeted messaging put social media platforms on the defensive. They also came under sustained attack from the right for 'anti-conservative' bias and suppression of right-wing content (Guynn, 2020; Sky News, 2019), despite these claims being baseless (Gabbatt, 2021), and despite Facebook teams operating inside the Trump campaign in 2016, training them in targeted messaging (Chafkin, 2022: 246). The effect was a defensive response by the liberal tech-elite, as they increasingly tried to please the ascendent right and, after 2021, to withdraw from political intervention, affiliation and even content to avoid government hostility and regulatory attention. Facebook, for example, burned by the issue of politics, re-oriented its news-feed algorithm towards groups and non-political content (Frenkel & Isaac, 2024).

By the time of the 2024 election, therefore, the 'liberal' technology elite had moved far away from open political expression due to their fear of the right. Hence, Bezos refused to let *The Washington Post* endorse a candidate, presumably afraid of angering Trump (Guardian Staff, 2024) and had Blue Origin meet with Trump soon after (Sainato, 2024), whilst a supplicatory Zuckerberg, having been threatened with jail if he interfered with the election, quickly visited Trump after his victory (Gerken, 2024b). Others who visited Trump included Sundar Pichai, Google's chief executive, Sergey Brin, a Google founder, Tim Cook, Apple's chief executive, and Jeff Bezos himself (Schleifer & Yaffe-Bellany, 2024). To confirm their support, Amazon, Meta and OpenAI each donated $1 m to Trump's inauguration fund (McMahon, 2024; Metz, 2024; Weise & Haberman, 2024).

By 2024, the 'liberal' bias of Silicon Valley had retreated and had even turned towards a radical, right-wing, anti-democratic philosophy. Consider Trump's political donors. In 2024, Silicon Valley skewed towards the populist right, donating over $394.1 m to Trump's campaign, with Elon Musk donating $243 m of this (Hernandes et al., 2024). Other tech-bro donors included Marc Andreessen ($5.5 m), Jan Koum ($5.1 m), Douglas Leone ($3.8 m), Benjamin Horowitz ($2.5 m), the Winklevoss twins ($2.5 m) and Jacob Helberg ($2.1 m). The 'tech-bros', and cryptocurrency investors, especially, all leaned towards Trump. As Carole Cadwalladr says, this was the ascendency of the 'broligarchy' (Cadwalladr, 2024c). The Obama-era (2009–2017) Silicon Valley devotion to the Democratic Party and liberal philosophy and causes was over. By 2024, the techno-elite had become explicitly and publicly aligned with the populist right.

The key figures in this capture were Marc Andreessen, Elon Musk and Peter Thiel. Marc Andreessen (1971–) is a businessman and former software engineer, perhaps best known for the creation of the Mosaic graphic browser creator and co-founder of Netscape, Opsware and Ning and the venture capitalist firm Andreessen-Horowitz, with a personal estimated net worth of £1.7 bn. Formerly a supporter of the Democratic Party, by 2024 he'd become a mega-donor to the political super-PAC and pro-cryptocurrency advocacy group Fairshake, favouring Trump and opposing Biden due to the possibility of higher taxes and stricter regulations on cryptocurrency and AI. In 2023, he published the right-wing, pro-Accelerationist, Transhumanist tract, 'The Techno-Optimist Manifesto' (Andreessen, 2023), advocating for a utopian vision of technology, favouring the neo-liberal market, 'the techno capital machine' and a libertarianism, with the hope of developments leading to us becoming 'technological supermen' (Andreessen, 2023).

Elon Musk (1971–) is the world's richest man, with an estimated wealth, by November 2024, of £310 bn. Born in South Africa, before moving to Canada, then the US, he was a co-founder of Zip2, an internet city-guide, which earned him $22 m when it was sold in 1999, and of X.com which, by 2000, would merge with PayPal, an online payments company that was bought by eBay for $1.5 bn in 2002, earning him $176 m. He went on to found SpaceX in 2002 and invested in Tesla in 2004, becoming CEO in 2008. In 2015, he co-founded the non-profit OpenAI; in 2016 he founded Neuralink; and in April 2022 he bought Twitter for $44 bn, rebranding it as X in 2023. Having left OpenAI in 2018 to avoid conflicts of interest, he founded XAI in March 2023. In California, Musk was registered as an independent voter and, although he has regularly donated to both Democrats and Republicans, his voting record was pro-Democrat. Musk voted for Obama in 2008 and 2012, for Hilary Clinton in 2016 and Joe Biden in 2020 (Feinberg, 2023) and even traded barbs with Trump in 2022 about his businesses. By then, however, Musk, who had already opposed coronavirus restrictions, was already moving decisively to the right and, in particular, to the conspiratorial, populist right.

Upon taking over Twitter, he significantly cut the staff, especially around content moderation, leading to a surge of unfiltered hate speech, and he even took out an unsuccessful law suit against an anti-hate speech group that highlighted this surge (Gerken, 2024a). He urged Americans to vote Republican in the 2022 mid-terms and endorsed Ron De Santis (Dorn, 2022); he reinstated the accounts of right-wing figures, previously banned for dangerous incitement (such as Trump, Marjorie Taylor Greene, Alex Jones, Jordan Peterson, Andrew Tate, Kanye West (Ye), Katie Hopkins and Tommy Robinson); he deactivated the accounts of certain journalists, and he began promoting his own pro-'free-speech', conspiratorial and anti-liberal-progressive views (Ivanova, 2022). In a tweet in November 2022, Musk made this anti-progressivism clear, claiming not to be right or left wing, but opposed to 'the woke mind-virus' that is 'pushing civilisation toward suicide' (Chantler Hicks, 2022).

By 2024, his pro-free-speech tweets had been embraced by the far-right in the UK, especially by the supporters of Reform, Nigel Farage and Tommy Robinson, though the fact that he acceded to censorship requests from Modi's India (TOI Tech Deck, 2024), that Saudi Arabia, with its poor record of human rights and speech rights, remains the second largest X investor (Al Jazeera, 2022) and that he sued advertisers who used their free-speech rights to remove themselves from X (Thomas & Fleury, 2024), pointed to the selective political choices Musk made on this issue. By August, the platform's promotion of far-right material contributed to the outburst of targeted violence and arson attacks at immigrants, Muslims and black people in the UK, which Musk then exploited, responding to far-right claims on X that 'mass migration and open borders' were to blame with the comment 'civil war is inevitable' in the UK. He also spread the far-right conspiracy theory about identitarian policing, by referring to '#TwoTierKier', taking a clear position both in the culture wars and in the far-right activism around immigration (Ziady, 2024). Responding to the UK prime minister's post about attacks on Muslim communities, Musk asked 'Shouldn't you be concerned about attacks on \*all\* communities?' He then repeated the remark in a tweet of his own, making allegations about violence from anti-racist and Muslim counter-protesters and accusing the police of a 'one-sided' approach (Spring, 2024).

He continued his attack on the UK government through 2024. In November, he taunted Starmer for his sinking approval ratings and questioned the imprisonment of Tommy Robinson, claiming Britain had become 'a tyrannical police state' (Clayton, 2024). By then many of the rioters and their supporters had been imprisoned, including, for example, Wayne O'Rourke who was jailed for 3 years for stirring up racial hatred. With 90,000 followers and a reach of up to 1.7 m people for his tweets, O'Rourke admitted earning £1400 a month from his account: hence X was explicitly supporting and financially-enabling the far-right and their rage (Mistry, 2024). Musk's support for the populist right would culminate domestically in his financial and political support for Donald Trump in November 2024. Trump's victory speech acknowledged the role of Musk, calling him 'a super genius' (Ray, 2024). Soon after, Musk's ascendency to the broligarchy was confirmed with Trump's announcement of Musk's new government role alongside Vivek Ramaswamy, leading the new presidential advisory committee, the Department of Government Efficiency ('DOGE'—a possibly deliberate reference to cryptocurrency). Its remit, of anti-bureaucratic cost-cutting, highlights its neo-liberal, pro-free-market origins and emphasis (Faguy & FitzGerald, 2024).

Peter Thiel (1967–) is an entrepreneur and venture capitalist with a personal wealth estimated in 2024 at $14.9 bn. Born in Germany, his parents moved to the US in 1968. After a temporary relocation to South Africa and South West Africa, his family settled in California in 1977. At Stanford University, he was already known for his right-wing politics. He read Ayn Rand and Rene Giraud, defended South African apartheid, expressed an early interest in extropianism (life-extension) and published the conservative, anti-liberal 'Stanford Review' (Chafkin, 2022: 18–27). His anti-liberal-progressivism found its clearest expression in his contribution to the 1990s 'culture wars', his publication in 1995 with David Sacks of *The Diversity Myth. Multiculturalism and Politics Intolerance on Campus*, which included anti-Feminist and homophobic commentary (Chafkin, 2022: 40–42).

After raising money to launch his venture capitalist career, he invested in Cofinity in 1998, an electronics payment company which launched PayPal in 1999 (which would merge with Musk's X.Com in 2000). By the time of eBay's purchase of PayPal in 2002, Thiel's stake was worth $55 m. Leaving the company, Thiel next set up the successful hedge fund Clarium Capital and was an early investor in Facebook in August 2004, with $500,000 bringing a 10.2% stake and a board seat. After the May 2012 IPO, he sold 16.8 m shares for $638 and then sold more shares in August for $400 m, with more share sales in 2016 and 2017 earning him another $100 m and $29 m. He remained on the (now) Meta board until 2022, when he left to campaign for Trumpian candidates in the midterm elections (Chapman et al., 2022). In May 2003, Thiel also founded Palantir, a big-data analytics company, and he remains its chairman. Its success came from its government contracts and use by the US intelligence community and Department of Defence, though it has since expanded its customer base to private companies and state and local government and international clients. As of December 2024, it had a market capitalisation of $173.21 bn.

Thiel's politics came to the fore again in his relationship with the Google engineer Patri Friedman, the grandson of the neo-liberal, monetarist economist Milton Friedman. Patri's libertarianism found expression in his blog and his interest in 'seasteading', or the creation of separate, sovereign, national governments on floating platforms in international waters. Thiel would fund his non-profit Seasteading Institute in 2008, with $500,000 (Chafkin 2022: 136–137). Continuing his extropian interests, he also invested $3 m into Aubrey De Gray's Methuselah Foundation and SENS Research Foundation from 2007 to 2010 and $1 m into the non-profit Singularity Institute (2022: 138–139). In the same period, Chafkin says, he was 'quietly cultivating a new crop of nativist politicians' and in 2008 made a $1 m donation to an anti-immigrant group (2022: 139). The following year he and Friedman contributed essays to an issue of *Cato Unbound* where, as we'll see, he expressed his anti-democratic views (2022: 140). His right-wing links, intellectually, economically and politically, continued to grow.

Thiel supported Trump in 2016, drawn to his anti-political correctness, anti-immigration and racist, nativist positions (around white identity), his claim that America was weak and in decline and his disruptive potential (Chafkin 2022: 226, 237). Thiel spoke at the July 2016 Republican

National Convention and donated $1.25 m to Trump's campaign (Stre-itfeld, 2016), becoming, after Trump's victory, a key voice in the early administration. He was given a role on the transition team and, seeing his job as disruptive of the deep-state bureaucracy, he explicitly put forward administrators 'who'd be inclined to gut the architecture of the New Deal and Great Society' (Chafkin, 2022: 250). The majority of his nomi-nations, however, weren't used. His attendance on nineteenth January 2017 at the 'DeploraBall', organised by his business-affiliate Jeff Giesea, confirmed his close links with the newly-emergent 'alt-right' movement. Palantir would benefit from new government contracts, including with ICE (the Immigration and Customs Enforcement Agency) and, in 2017, Thiel would invest in Clearview, a facial-recognition company that would be used by US police and by ICE (2022: 267–268). Palantir also benefited from Google's withdrawal from defence work, following an employee backlash, whilst Thiel's investment in the defence contractor Anduril also paid off, with the company providing support for the Customs and Border Protection agency (2022: 290, 285).

Though Thiel would gradually distance himself from Trump, he remained connected to the broader conservative and alt-right movement and to anti-political correctness. In July 2019, he was the headline speaker at the National Conservatism Conference in Washington, alongside J.D. Vance. Vance had first met Thiel in 2011 when he was a student at Yale Law School and Thiel had given a speech at the university (Mansfield, 2024). Thiel had given Vance a job in his venture capitalist firm Mithril Capital, and Vance had broken out with his 2016 memoir of Appalachian culture, *Hillbilly Elegy* (Vance, 2017). Thiel then helped launch his polit-ical career, giving his Ohio US Senate race campaign $15 m, which he won (Mansfield, 2024). In 2021, Vance and Thiel both invested in the conservative video platform Rumble (Hagey, 2021), which would go on to become a major right-wing influencer platform and news-source in the 2024 election (Thompson, 2024). Though Vance had criticised Trump in 2016, it was Thiel that introduced them at Mar-a-Lago in the Spring of 2021 (Chafkin, 2022: 332). By then, Thiel's support for Trump had returned. In July 2024, Trump would pick Vance as his vice-presidential nominee: it would ensure a continued inner-circle connection to the 47th President of the US.

What we can draw from this, therefore, is the withdrawal of the liberal tech-elite from politics, scared by the ascendent right and put off by a growing Democratic Party interest in regulation for social harms. Instead, key tech figures pivoted explicitly to the populist right and to a pro-Trumpian position. What they have in common with the mass of Trump voters is a social conservativism that opposes liberal-progressivism and its identity politics and a strong anti-liberal-democratic sentiment. The opposition of each to democracy, however, has a very different basis, motivation and demand.

## THE PHILOSOPHY OF EXIT

There are many strands of right-wing and conservative thought in post-war America. The broligarchy draws on a range of sources, framed around several key ideas—neo-liberalism, the Randian hero, libertarianism and anti-democracy and the failure of the Western liberal political system. In particular, we can identify a series of authors and critics that have especially inspired the political positions taken by the new, right-wing tech-elite.

The first of these is the continued influence of Friedrich Hayek. Along with Ludwig Von Mises, he represents the intellectual foundation of neo-liberal thought, in advocating a libertarian, individualist political philosophy and an economic philosophy of free markets. Though neo-liberalism is often framed (as we have done in the previous chapter) as fundamentally anti-statist, in reality it has often allied itself with a strong, conservative state (Gamble, 1989) and relied on strong institutions at the global level to support its marketisation (Slobodian, 2018). More precisely, as Hayek's 1944 book *The Road to Serfdom* makes clear, the actual target of neo-liberal wrath is 'collectivism', or the economically interventionist, redistributive state (Hayek, 2001: 35–36).

Hayek's book was a reaction against this state, as represented by the US New Deal response to the Great Depression in the 1930s, the totalitarian systems of German Fascism and USSR Communism, and the war-time state direction of the Allied economies. It was a warning too against the emerging 'socialist' expansion of these policies by Allied powers in the post-war period (2001: 205–206) and Hayek would devote the following decades to opposing this post-war Western, Keynesian redistributive system in favour of the free market. He was a founder member of the Mont Pelerin Society in 1947 and he promoted the development of international think tanks to oppose this interventionist state and wage what Stedman Jones calls 'an ideological war' for neo-liberalism (Stedman Jones, 2012: 135). What's important to grasp is that for Hayek in 1944 all interventionist states *are the same*, in their collectivist orientation, their replacement of the market with central 'planning' and their reversal of the 'individualist civilisation' the west was built upon (2001: 14).

Remarkably, therefore, for Hayek all collectivist states, whether totalitarian or welfare-based, represent an *identical* form of slavery—'the high road to servitude' (2001: 27). This is his greatest error as, in reality, Western post-war Keynesianism was very different to totalitarianism, representing instead, for many, a 'golden age' in which the worst effects of laisser-faire capitalism were ameliorated and social provision and care represented a positive form of liberty, enabling populations to live better lives, with health, education and a social security safety net. Conflating welfare-capitalism with repressive, terror-based totalitarianism was fundamentally indefensible, representing a deliberate ideological attack on all economics that weren't laisser-faire.

Today's tech-elite, therefore, continue in their neo-liberal faith in unregulated, globally-operating free markets and their opposition to state regulation, but they also retain this Hayekian fear of the redistributive state helping the population. Because the people, for them, are not really *people*, but self-maximising, free-individuals and should be treated as such, with any failures representing their own, personal choices. Hence Musk's comment on homelessness in a December 2024 tweet, saying 'In most cases, the word "homeless" is a lie. It's usually a propaganda word for violent drug addicts with severe mental illness' (Peat, 2024; Woodward, 2024). The philosophy of *neo-liberal exit* originates with Hayek—as an exit from 'the monster state' (Hayek, 2001: 223) and from society, the 'public' and responsibility for them. It's popular with the tech-elite because their individualism is not just Hayekian, it is also fundamentally Randian.

Ayn Rand, the script-writer, author and theorist, is known today for her anti-communism and anti-collectivism, her embrace of neo-liberal free markets and her 'objectivist' ethical philosophy which venerated 'rational egoism', seeing self-interest as natural and altruism as against life (Rand, 1964). As she said in 1957, 'My philosophy, in essence, is the concept of man as a heroic being, with his own happiness as the moral purpose of his life, with productive achievement as his noblest activity, and reason as his only absolute' (2007b: 1170–1171). Though outside of established academia and philosophy, she developed a devoted following and her novels and essays have had a significant influence upon right-wing US neo-liberal and libertarian thought (see Duggan, 2019; Heller, 2009). Most of the Silicon Valley tech-bros had read Rand and her influence upon 'the Californian Ideology' (Barbrook & Cameron, 1995) has been widely noted. Her influence upon the new wave of *broligarchical* figures, however, needs to be re-emphasised, as they see themselves as the leading men she valued.

In her novels *The Fountainhead* in 1943 (Rand, 2007a) and *Atlas Shrugged* in 1957 (Rand, 2007b), Rand presents us with heroic, capitalist, individualist, world-making ubermensch—Harold Roark and John Galt—who are the real innovators in society: the only truly productive individuals and worthy men. In her novels, she distinguishes between 'bureaucrats' and 'builders', contrasting collectivist rules with the energy and genius of the individual-seer, the 'men of talent' who are 'the motor of the world' (Freedland, 2017). In *Atlas Shrugged,* she even has this elite react against government regulations and control by going on strike, with John Galt encouraging other builders *to exit society*, leaving them to their own fate, to build their own productive life in his neo-liberal, utopian, gulch free from the parasitical altruists, the looters and moochers, the expropriators and the 'needy' (Heller, 2009: 195). Rand's ideas flatter the tech-elite, therefore, as they see themselves in these leading men—as alpha-male, visionary, creative geniuses who make and remake the world at will, with no thought for the lesser people and their desires or demands. Steve Jobs, Mark Zuckerberg (with his mantra of 'move fast and break things'), Travis Kalanick (of Uber), Elon Musk and Peter Thiel have all identified with these Randian heroes, whilst Trump himself has praised *The Fountainhead* (Freedland, 2017). In his speech at the 2016 Republican National Convention Peter, Thiel explicitly described himself as 'a builder', like Trump (Chafkin, 2022: 238). Following Hayek and Rand, the logic goes, these are all men who surely should be doing *anything they want*, as the truly brilliant people, instead of being held back by a regulatory state and, implicitly, by democracy and the levelling rule of the masses. And if we do hold them back, surely they have a Galtian right of exit?

This concept of 'exit' has become increasingly important on the right. It was most explicitly developed by the German economist Albert O. Hirschman, whose 1970 book *Exit, Voice and Loyalty* has proven especially influential in economics, business studies and for the right (Hirschman, 1970). The book is ostensibly about businesses, though the sub-title—'Responses to decline in firms, organizations and states'—indicates it has broader political implications. Faced with a decline in satisfaction with a service or goods, Hirschman argues, customers have two primary options. They can speak up and protest and try to change the company and its practices from within (the political action of using their 'voice'), or they can leave for a better competitor (the economic option of 'exit'). The latter is especially important, as the 'invisible hand' of the market is best placed, he says, to aid the recovery of the firm (1970: 15–16), though this is complicated where there is intense 'loyalty', which encourages people to focus especially on voice for change. Hirschman's book includes brief discussions of the problem of the state, as there 'the exit option is unavailable' as no competition is available. In this case, he argues, the option of voice is most pronounced in response (1970: 33). It was precisely this issue of state monopoly, however, that would fascinate the US right. What if, they reasoned, there *could* be competition?

Hirschman's book is often read now alongside another related title, James Dale Davidson and William Rees-Mogg's 1997 book, *The Sovereign Individual* which has become perhaps *the* key text of the broligarchy. Thiel, especially, embraced the book and provided a preface for its 2020 reprint (Davidson and Rees-Mogg, 2020: 5–6). On the one level, the book is completely obsolete in seeing cyberspace as a separate world apart. It was published the year after John Perry Barlow's 'Declaration of the Independence of Cyberspace' (Barlow, 1996), which characterised the online world as a non-physical domain, 'the new home of mind', which was removed from all forms of government authority and means of control. The best description of this era comes in Erik Davis' 1998 book *Techgnosis*, where he compares contemporary ideas about cyberspace to religious (and especially Gnostic) conceptions of the division between the real, physical world and a higher, immaterial soul-space floating free of the world (Davis, 1998). In fact, in the decade following *The Sovereign Individual*'s publication, the most important developments in digital technology were the implosion of 'cyberspace' with material, everyday life (with broadband, Wi-Fi, improved phone systems and the smartphone) and the growing success of governments in imposing controls within their borders over its operation and online behaviours (Goldsmith & Wu, 2006). Despite this, however, there is much that Davidson and Rees-Mogg do get right, and the book is better read today as a blueprint for what today's tech-elite *want to be the case* and *what they want to be able to do*.

Davidson and Rees-Mogg's book begins with a retread of standard post-industrial theory by positing our entry into 'a new stage of history' called 'the information age': a fourth stage of social organisation following hunter-gathering, agriculture and industrialism (Davidson & Rees-Mogg, 2020: 14–15). The main feature of this new era they say—somewhat glee-fully, as neo-liberals—is 'the death of the modern nation state' (2020: 42) as this 'exhausted' form (2020: 15) is undermined by new technology (2020: 99) in a 'megapolitical earthquake' (2020: 37). This will lead us—within our lifetime (2020: 17)—into 'a new stage in Western civil-isation' (2020: 52) in which the old, 'protection racket' of the industrial state loses its ability to extort money from the wealthy and successful (2020: 162, 176). There are many changes that Davidson and Rees-Mogg presciently predict, including the 'metaverse', virtual communities, 'information warfare' and 'cyberwar', AI chatbots and assistants, phone-banking, remote work, customised media and information, etc. (2020: 30, 30, 43, 70, 172, 206, 204, 205, 255, 360), but their main focus is on the liberation of the economy and hence of the individual.

The coming era will see the explosion of the 'cybereconomy', they say (2020: 19, 179). With business being conducted now from anywhere (2020: 21), with capital more mobile (2020: 21), with the growth of independent 'cybercurrencies' beyond state control (2020: 24) and with strong encryption (2020: 194, 212), cyberspace will be 'the ultimate offshore jurisdiction' (2020: 24). With the assets of the wealthy now beyond reach (2020: 155), states will be starved of (redistributive) tax income and hence of the ability to milk their 'cows' (2020: 24). The cybereconomy will see the rise of virtual corporations (2020: 159), in a space beyond territory, where there is less state control (2020: 159–160) and little union power (2020: 170). This will all incentivise and empower those neo-liberal, Randian heroes best able to take advantage of this new regime, unleashing their 'genius' from the shackles of states, creating 'sovereign individuals' (2020: 18), who, like 'gods' (2020: 18), will turn ideas into wealth (2020: 18) and reconfigure the world (2020: 20). They will form a 'denationalised' (2020: 295) and globalised 'infor-mation elite' (2020: 297) and 'world super-class' (2020: 388) who will follow 'the morality of the information age', which will be 'the morality of the market' (2020: 392).

With borders obsolete (2020: 23, 178, 187), we will see an explo-sion of sovereignties (2020: 190, 257), of new sovereign 'cities' (2020: 16), with 'the genuine privatisation of sovereignty' (2020: 321) and the commercial provision of government services (2020: 190, 204), with competition (2020: 244) now allowing Hirschman's option of 'exit'

(2020: 243, 268, 297) as sovereign individuals 'shop ... among juris-
dictions' (2020: 212). Citizenship, therefore, is erased, with 'citizens'
replaced by 'customers' (2020: 263), in a final, neo-liberal dream that will
see the end of taxation—'the exploitation of the capitalists by the workers' (2020: 161)—as well as trade unions (2020: 155), welfare spending
and income redistribution (2020: 135, 233) and the 'nanny state' (2020:
279). Extranational, mobile, global identities will rule (2020: 292–293),
with any economic power able to launch its own proprietary ministate
(2020: 336), such that 'In a better world, every successful head of
government would be a multimillionaire' (2020: 340).

One obvious—and, for them, desired—result would be the end of
industrial-era 'mass-democracy' (2020: 142). 'Representative democracy',
they argue, 'will fade away, to be replaced by the new democracy of
choice in the cybermarketplace' (2020: 42). In part, this will be due to
economics, as the underachieving (2020: 345) mass of the public will
no longer be able to use the state to exploit the talented wealthy who
will simply 'exit'. The information age, therefore, will be characterised by
a 'more elitist and less egalitarian age' (2020: 227), as those with rarer
and more valued skills and the most 'ambitious' and talented around the
globe will benefit, leading to increased inequality within nations (2020:
231, 237–238). There will, however, be 'legions of losers' (2020: 257)
in the information age, and for a time there will be anger, resentment
and violence from the 'left-behinds' (2020: 301). The loss of the nation
state will lead, Davidson and Rees-Mogg argue, to 'an intense and even
violent nationalist reaction' among those who lose 'status', including an
'opposition to globalisation' and 'hostility to immigration' (2020: 260).
There will a growing tension between the small, elite 'information aristocracy' and the 'growing underclass' of the 'information poor' (2020:
269). Tribalized (2020: 311), prone to a violent backlash (2020: 309)
and resistant to innovation (2020: 315), these will be our contemporary
'neo-Luddites' (2020: 318) who will even resort to terrorism against the
new world (2020: 319).

The contemporary relevance of these ideas will already be obvious, but
first they would be refracted through another right-wing movement: that
of 'accelerationism' and 'The Dark Enlightenment'. Accelerationism is the
belief that a current situation or society should be sped up and intensified
in order to break through and progress. Many trace its roots to Marx's
*The Communist Manifesto*, and the desire to push through capitalism
towards the revolutionary future (Hoffman & Ware, 2024: 3), and the

idea has occasionally inspired contemporary left-wing forms of techno-futurist accelerationism (Srnicek & Williams, 2013, 2015). Its primary modes of expression today, however, have been on the right and far-right. On a practical level, perhaps Charles Manson and his 1969 attempts to start a race-war by framing black people for murder can be seen as a key figure in far-right accelerationism (see Bugliosi, 2018), whilst Hoffman and Ware identify the US militia movements and domestic right-wing terrorists as subscribing to a similar accelerationist ideology (Hoffman & Ware, 2024: 1–12). The term, itself, however, picked up by Noys in 2010 and first appearing in Zelazny's 1967 novel *Lord of Light* (Noys, 2014: xi) is more associated today with a particular theory—a brand of techno-futurist, pro-neo-liberal, racist, anti-Western Enlightenment, anti-liberal-democratic, right-wing thought, best seen in the work of Curtis Yarvin and Nick Land (see Burrows, 2018; Smith & Burrows, 2021; Farrell, 2024).

Curtis Yarvin (1973–) is an American blogger. Having dropped out of a computing PhD at UC Berkeley, to join a tech company, he went on to found the decentralised computer platform Urbit in 2002 and cofound Tlön Corp with funding from Thiel's founder's fund, which brought him into a personal relationship with the venture capitalist. His fame, however, comes from his blog 'Unqualified Reservations' which ran from 2007 to 2014 under the name 'Mencius Moldbug'. (Since 2020 he has published his 'Gray Mirror' on Substack.) Drawing on Thomas Carlyle, Ludwig Von Mises, James Burnham and Hans-Hermann Hoppe's 2001 book *Democracy: The God That Failed* (Hoppe, 2017), Yarvin has argued that US democracy is a failed experiment that needs to be replaced by a new authoritarianism: an accountable neo-monarchy with a corporate governance structure. This would be a techno-monarchy modelled on Prussian cameralism, where the state was conceived as a business that owned the country. His ideas became known as Neo-Cameralism', then 'Neo-Reactionism' ('NRx'). Anti-democracy, 'exit', new corporate governance structures, free city-states beyond government authority selling citizenship: the same themes repeat, but with the addition now into the mix of an interest in monarchical power and a definite turn towards authoritarianism and dictatorship.

Perhaps Yarvin's most famous concept is 'the Cathedral' (Yarvin, 2022). Famously first theorised by Eric Raymond in his defence of 'open-source' software, where it was used to contrast bottom-up software creation with that of major companies like Microsoft (Raymond,

1998), with Yarvin it became the centre of a broader, societal, right-wing conspiracy theory. Yarvin takes up Raymond's distinction between the 'bazaar', described here as 'an open, volunteer, centreless, organic community', and the 'cathedral', which is 'any centralised organisation' with 'a single purpose'. Employing Gaetano Mosca, Yarvin argues that within state sovereignty, 'there is one *official* culture: the people who govern, plus the people who think like them'. To succeed, sovereignty must ensure psychological as well as physical consent, engineering the minds of the public through political formula. That suggests some kind of Orwellian state, hence, 'a literal cathedral', but today, Yarvin says, the public 'see no such regimented organisation. They can buy all the ideas they want at any stall in the bazaar. Therefore—despite the evidence of their eyes—they conclude that their minds are free'. However, despite coming from any stall, the ideas we consume 'all seem to come from the same manufacturer – exactly as if made in some cathedral'. Hence, we have a bazaar spontaneously organising itself to behave as a cathedral.

Yarvin's explanation for this is the failure of the marketplace of ideas, due to its poisoning and domination by 'mainstream journalism' and 'prestigious academia', who have been captured by the (liberal) elite and turned into government agencies. Journalism now becomes 'the Information Department' of government, and academia and science 'the Truth Department'. These two 'camouflaged departments' add up to 'a Department of Reality which is unquestionably the center of power in our regime'. It is, however, a decentralised one, able to permeate everyday life, such that in the marketplace 'all the stores sell the same ideas'. Hence Yarvin's conclusion is that 'the bazaar evolved into a cathedral'. Channelling Aristotle, Yarvin somewhat confusingly argues that today we are living in an 'oligarchy' (which he defines—counter-intuitively—as our democracy), suggesting that we have one of two other Aristotelian models left, either 'democracy' (defined by him as 'populism') or 'monarchy' (or 'dictatorship'). For Yarvin, the latter is our preferred future: as he says, 'human history's most common form of government by far is still out there—waiting for us to get tired of living the way we live now'.

Yarvin's concept of 'the Cathedral' would be embraced by the right as a collective, overall term for the 'deep-state' attacked by QAnon, the 'fake news media' attacked by Trump and the entire 'mainstream' rejected now and raged against by the right and far-right and those captured by their rhetoric and ideas. The public bought into an anti-liberal-democratic theory pushed by an elitist, pro-dictatorial, pro-corporate monarchist *exit-theorist*, enfolding it within their sharded media realities and conspiratorial mindset, to oppose the entire liberal, mainstream 'department of reality'. Yarvin's influence has grown massively, not only through his personal links with Thiel, but also through his impact on J.D. Vance's thinking and on many others newly installed in the Trump administration, including Michael Anton who promotes a similar idea of authoritarian 'Caesarism' (Wilson, 2024). But Yarvin had another fan, with his work being promoted by and joined by that of the English philosopher Nick Land and his concept of 'The Dark Enlightenment'.

Nick Land (1962–) was originally known for his work with the 'Cybernetic Culture Research Unit' (CCRU) which he and Sadie Plant founded at the University of Warwick. From 1995, until its dissolution in 2003, it offered one of the most exciting, radical interpretations of the then-burgeoning cyberculture, incorporating post-structuralist theory (Deleuze and Guattari and Lyotard), cybernetics, Marxism, critical theory, situationism, futurism, nihilism, complexity theory, numerology, Gothic horror, demonology, jungle music and cyberpunk, all explored through its publications and activities such as the 'Virtual Futures' conferences (see Beckett, 2017; CCRU, 2017; Land, 2011; Noys, 2014). By the time of its collapse, however, it had descended into a 'quasi-cultish or quasi-religious' group (Beckett, 2017), becoming disaffiliated from the University and disappearing into ever more esoteric interests. Afterwards, Land would disappear, until long into the new millennium, moving to Taiwan, then Shanghai, publishing his now overtly-racist and right-wing accelerationist ideas online where they would find a receptive American audience.

*The Dark Enlightenment* is his best-known posting, a dense, not always comprehensible, 28,000 word document from December 2012 (Land, 2023). Here he takes aim at liberalism and its 'Enlightenment', developing his earlier post-modernist, post-structuralist cyber-cultural critique into a sustained, politically-inspired, right-wing rejection of reason, 'the egalitarian hypothesis', individual rights and democracy itself and an implicit promotion of Enlightenment's 'dark' opposite. His neoreactionary philosophy, therefore, 'coincides exactly with the expectation that democracy will die messily, as the popular degeneration of the liberal social order proceeds' (2023: x). The first part of his text is a collage of the ideas discussed above, quoting extensively from the Hirschman-inspired 'exit-voice' debate (suggesting exit as the only option now for libertarians), and name-dropping and discussing the ideas of Thiel, Patri

Friedman, Hoppe and Yarvin—'the incandescent genius' (2023: 13). Here, like Davidson and Rees-Mogg, he accuses democracy of plundering society and holding back (and even consuming) material progress (2023: 6, 17) and destroying freedom (2023: 14); like Yarvin, he condemns 'the Cathedral' and its 'comprehensive thought-control' (2023: 12); and, like the right generally, he complains of the woke rise of 'Grievance Studies departments' at 'New England universities' (2023: 12).

If there is a new element he explicitly introduces it is his obsession with race, in his rejection of equality and his promotion of 'human biological diversity' (2023: 22)—a now common right-wing, euphemistic trope ('HBD'). In the latter part of the book, Land continually attacks the 'Universalist democratic-egalitarian faith' that we are all equal (2023: 34), an idea he rejects:

> Human inequality ... in all its abundant multiplicity, is constantly on display as people exhibit their variations in gender, ethnicity, physical attractiveness, size and shape, strength, health, agility, charm, humor, wit, industriousness, sociability, among countless other feature, traits, abilities and aspects of their personality ... People are not equal, they do not develop equality, their goals and achievements are not equal, and nothing can make them equal. (Land, 2023: 60–61)

Land devotes his rage to this new 'authoritarian religion' and its commandment to 'accept progressive social policy as the *only possible* solution to the sin problem of inequality' (2023: 61). He rails against 'political correctness' and how 'progressive-universalistic beliefs about human nature' are held as 'religious tenets' that it is 'heresy' to question (2023: 22), with this 'supreme and defining social sin' courting 'universal condemnation' for its 'thought-crimes' (2023: 22). Racism, here, '*is pure or absolute evil*' (2023: 22).

Much of this is the standard right-wing gripe against liberal-progressivism, and 'the assertive multiculturalism' of our 'soft-totalitarian democracy' (2023: 27) where all unwanted speech is condemned as 'hate' (2023: 28–29). He describes this universalist-progressivism as a 'cult' (2023: 34)—one which spreads with 'an epidemic virulence that is disguised as progressive enlightenment' (2023: 34). For Land, it is this cult that seems to lie at the core of 'the Cathedral' which, he says, 'extends and tightens its grip upon everything, everywhere' (2023: 34), having now 'ascended to global supremacy' (2023: 35). Somehow, Land's target, liberal-progressivism, comes to take on a world-leading significance. By the end, he sees it establishing a 'New Jerusalem in Washington' with a 'master narrative' for the world; a 'Messianic revolutionary purpose' which aims 'to install a new world order of universal fraternity, in the name of equality, human rights, social justice and – above all – *democracy*' (2023: 88–89). Like Davidson and Rees-Mogg and Yarvin, however, Land is convinced that this mass-democracy will fail, due, he says, to the 'gluttonous consumption' (2023: 88) of 'the cancerous entitlement state' (2023: 84). However, his repeated assertion of democracy's 'degeneration' (2023: 30) hits differently given the repeated focus through the rest of the book on race, inequality and IQ, just as his discussion of exit and 'the coming crack-up' (2023: 82) has uncomfortable echoes of ethno-nationalist ideas.

All the ideas and authors of these movements seem to be pushing in the same direction. We can add to them the accelerationist ideas of Marc Andreessen's 2023 'Techno-Optimist Manifesto', and the work of Balaji S. Srinivasan (1980–), an American entrepreneur and investor, the co-founder of Counsyl, a genetic testing firm, the former Chief Technology Officer of Coinbase, a cryptocurrency exchange platform, and former general partner of Marc at the Andreesen Horowitz venture capitalist firm. In 2013, Srinivasan gave a speech entitled 'Silicon Valley's Ultimate Exit' (Srinivasan, 2013) in which he discussed the 'exit-voice' debate and postulated a new form of exit from government controls, with Silicon Valley building its own 'opt-in society, ultimately outside the US, run by technology'. He followed it up with a self-published, Hirschman-inspired book in 2022 entitled *The Network State* (Srinivasan, 2022), exploring how to exit from geographical governments, with digital communities crowd-funding resources to build autonomous cities and states. *Exit*, therefore, is now the key right-wing broligarchical trope. But it is *not* what the people want.

## THE PEOPLE VS THE ELITE

What the people and the elite share, in their Trumpianism, is an anti-liberal-progressivism and an anti-liberal-democratic sentiment. It seems that the social conservativism that winces at 'woke' identitarian ideas and minority support is a shared sentiment of both the Trumpian, status-threatened public and the status-enhanced elite, but what their anti-democratic sentiment means is very different. For the people, their anti-democratic rage is aimed at the *withdrawal* of the state. They resent the political withdrawal of politicians from the real lives, problems and pain of the public—their distance, professionalisation and service to the system—and they resent the economic withdrawal from the US by a global neo-liberalism that leaves them behind as poor consumers of cheap global goods brought to them by IT-coordinated containers from the industrialised developing world, rather than as life-long, meaningfully-employed workers, earning a living-wage and living within established, thriving communities. What do they want from the liberal-democratic state, therefore? *They want re-entry.* They want it to re-focus domestically, to look towards them, to reinvest in their lives and work and care. They want the state to go back to actually representing them. They never wanted participatory democracy—who has the time for that?—but they *do* want the return of a representative democracy that genuinely tries to represent them and for whom their domestic issues are paramount.

This is where the tech-elite differ. They, too, are anti-liberal-democratic, but only because they want *a final, radicalised exit* from the representative state. Unlike the voided, left-behind public, they remain *pro-global-neo-liberalism* and hence their response to the redistributive, interventionist, regulatory, protectionist state and its 'positive' liberty is completely different: *they want rid of it (and of the people) with exit*. And none of this has ever been hidden. As we've seen, all of the key right-wing thinkers and commentators were openly saying this for decades, aligning on this, pushing the same neo-liberal, accelerationist goal, *beyond* the democratic state that the people desperately want back. A shared, Trumpian anti-democracy, therefore, leads in two distinct directions: whilst the people hope for re-entry, the tech-elite dream of exit.

This is Hayek and the exit from the 'socialist' state—from the connective, communitarian 'social' and its taxation, redistribution and welfare *care* for everyone. This is Rand and the exit from the 'bureaucrats' and the leechers and moochers dragging down the geniuses who should be free from rules, constraints and obligations to the masses. This is Hirschman and the competitive, economic exit from a state with its declining services and satisfaction for those with economic power. This is Davidson and Rees-Mogg and exit from geographical territory, state sovereignty and the forced 'protection racket' that robs the wealthy, in favour of privatised city-state sovereignty and preferential customer-service for the rich. This is Yarvin and exit, again, for free-roaming city-state sovereignty and from the dominant deep-state political and liberal thought-control of the mainstream 'Cathedral'. This is Land and exit from the 'cult' of equality and the forced acceptance of the racially inferior. This is Andreesen and Srinivasan too, and exit ever more completely from everything that previously bound us together in the industrial-era. The hope for disruption, therefore, is fundamentally shared by the Trumpian public and the elite, but it is also fundamentally *opposed*. The public want to disrupt contemporary democracy in order to bring it *back to them*; the elite want to disrupt democracy in order *to leave it behind* in favour of an accelerated global neo-liberalism.

Consider again Musk and Thiel. Any liberal-democratic sentiment Musk might have had is long-gone. Now he aligns himself with the US and UK populist right and far-right, pretending to sympathise with them, but actually he is using them to help promote the destruction of liberal-democratic systems. This is, arguably, the reason why he bought Twitter in the first place. Though far from perfect, it did have the rare reputation of remaining a key, digital, Habermasian, essentially liberal, 'public sphere' for journalism and commentary, for the democratic education and informing of the public, for holding authorities to account and for enabling the sharing of information and hosting of debate. In buying it, ridding it of moderation, allowing right-wing accounts to return and hate speech and disinformation to proliferate, Musk achieved the 'enshittification' (Doctorow, 2023) of a valuable digital, pro-democratic commons. Though here enshittification wasn't intended to further exploit its advertisers or users (as Doctorow means the term), but rather, following Putin, to introduce a chaos that undermines liberal debate and democratic politics. Whereas liberalism wants an ordered, rational-critical public sphere, the right wants one based on the chaotic flinging of shit.

Musk, as Vaidhyanathan suggests, 'is the ultimate chaos agent' (Vaidhyanathan, 2024). On 20th December 2024, this unelected figure called for the US House of Representatives to reject the negotiated continuing resolution that it had to pass to keep the federal government funded:

> "This bill should not pass," the richest human being in the world wrote at 4.15am ET. Musk followed up for hours, using every derogatory word he could muster to describe a bill he almost certainly had not read nor understood. "Any member of the House or Senate who votes for this outrageous spending bill deserves to be voted out in 2 years!" Musk wrote Wednesday afternoon. (Vaidhyanathan, 2024)

Musk has no interest in the democratic functioning of the US, he is only interested in how he *wants it to operate*, preferably in *his* political and economic interests. He wants an anti-democratic US functioning in support of the Randian super-rich. This is the opposite of what his MAGA and Reform supporters want.

So, Musk now promotes himself as a friend of MAGA and Reform, but he's also the richest person in the world. He is the Randian hero and why should the voice or vote of another, lower person be worth the same as his? He is the innovative, creative 'builder' for whom democracy represents the 'bureaucrats' and the unproductive. Does he really share, therefore, the same politics as the UK Reform supporters he defends? No, he wants them to hasten—to accelerate—political violence and chaos, not for a re-entry of the democratic system into their lives as they want, but for a final exit from a system that takes their tiny lives, opinions and votes seriously. Musk is *anti* the populist right wing he promotes. He is contemptuous of the little person. And he remains committed most of all to *exit*—to exit from democratic oversight and government regulation and to exit from the entire earth itself and its lesser human populations, with his spending on SpaceX and hopes for a Mars colony (Luscombe, 2024). Even Bezos sees space travel as a liberatory future for a select mankind (Massie, 2021). In the 1980s, a right-wing 'transhumanism' developed that saw the future as leaving physical humanity behind, to 'download' oneself into a digital reality dominated, as Moravec suggested, by a neo-liberal market economy in which you had to earn your processing power (Kurzweil, 2005; Moravec, 1988). Today's transhumanist tech-gurus promote a different, Galtian, human physical exit—from the public, from the state and from the entire planet.

Musk's anti-democracy was also made explicit on 20th December 2024 with his tweet, 'Only the AfD can save Germany'. He reposted a video by a German right-wing influencer, Naomi Seibt, who criticised Friedrich Merz, the leader of the conservative Christian Democrats and also praised Javier Milei, the libertarian president of Argentina (Connolly, 2024). This was the active support of Neo-Nazism, versus the processes of parliamentary democracy. On the same day, a report suggested that Musk and Ramaswamy's new Department of Government Efficiency (DOGE) would intentionally cut entitlement programmes so that Trump could 'ram through massive tax giveaways for the ultra-wealthy and corporations' (Owens, 2024). What it exposed was DOGE's aim to cut public spending, to enable pro-global neo-liberal tax-cuts, all of which oppose the nativist, protectionist hopes of ordinary, anti-global-neo-liberal voters. Meanwhile, Musk continues to benefit financially from these government economic processes (Isidore, 2024). A day later, on 21ˢᵗ December, an ADF supporter who had expressed support for Musk carried out a car attack on the Magdeburg Christmas market, killing 5 and injuring hundreds (Cole, 2024).

Peter Thiel remains enmeshed within all these figures and currents, as the backstage friend and financier of so many key, right-wing individuals and organisations. His socially-conservative, anti-liberal-progressivism was well known, but his anti-democratic sentiment became explicit in his 2009 *Cato Unbound* contribution, 'The Education of a Libertarian' (Thiel, 2009). The essay opens with an explanation of his beliefs:

> I remain committed to the faith of my teenage years: to authentic human freedom as a precondition for the highest good. I stand against confiscatory taxes, totalitarian collectives, and the ideology of the inevitability of the death of every individual. For all these reasons, I still call myself "libertarian." (Thiel, 2009)

But, he adds, over the last two decades he has changed his mind as to how this should be achieved, explaining that, 'I no longer believe that freedom and democracy are compatible' (Thiel, 2009).

Describing his political journey he admits that, by 2009, 'the prospects for a libertarian politics appear grim indeed', as the response to the 2008 crash will inevitably involve 'more government'. He lauds the response to the 1920–1921 depression in avoiding that government role, but immediately complains about the inflated state since, and in particular 'the vast increase in welfare beneficiaries and the extension of the franchise to women'. This should cause despair for the libertarian, he suggests, but there is now a solution, as politics no longer encompasses 'all possible futures of our world'. In particular, we now have the option of finding 'an escape' from politics by going 'beyond it'. He considers three technological exits. One of these is Davidson and Rees-Mogg's stateless cyberspace beyond government control (and, indeed, he reminds us that this was the original libertarian, anti-statist intention of PayPal); the next option is space travel, and the possibility of leaving the planet behind (with SpaceX); and the third is 'seasteading', or the settlement of the seas (included here as he'd just invested in Friedman's Seasteading Institute).

His essay ends with a Randian celebration of the builder who might be able to solve the problem of politics: 'The fate of our world may depend on the effort of a single person who builds or propagates the machinery of freedom that makes the world safe for capitalism' (Thiel, 2009).

So, how did we get from this in 2009 to the Trumpian Thiel in 2016 and 2024? How do you go from an avowed exit-libertarian to supporting authoritarianism, which is the exact opposite political position? It only makes sense when we understand Thiel's hatred of democracy as the linking thread. Democracy, for him, represents collectivism, bureaucracy, rules, regulations, constraints and controls on neo-liberal business as well as taking seriously the lives, needs and opinions of the masses, according each of them individual value and providing for them with the money taken by taxation. If *that* is what you oppose, and if it turns out your hopes of exit to a stateless cyberspace, to space colonies or sovereign sea-cities were too naïve, then what do you turn to? If you can't escape politics and you realise that libertarianism will never be powerful enough to oppose democracy, then what might be? It's at that point that you turn to a suitably Randian, authoritarian figure with the power to make what you want happen. Hence the pivot of Thiel and the libertarian, pro-global-neo-liberalism tech-bros towards a figure free enough to support their businesses and strong enough and angry enough to take down the structures, procedures and powers of democratic government. Libertarianism, it turns out, has a closer affinity with authoritarianism than with social democracy: they're both built on the sovereign will of the privileged, heroic individual.

Curtis Yarvin has openly discussed how that attack on democracy could be achieved (Wilson, 2024). In a May 2021 recording with Michael Anton for the Claremont Institute's 'The American Mind podcast', he explained his position that an authoritarian should campaign from the start on that explicit, honest platform, and then, when they get power, they should declare a state of emergency in their inaugural address. With a mandate, that would be possible and also lawful. Then you'd follow that up with taking down the enemies that oppose you, especially 'the Cathedral'. As Yarvin says, 'you can't continue to have a Harvard or a *New York Times* past since perhaps the start of April'. As he clarified, you can't take power and function 'with someone else's Department of Reality in operation'. Chillingly, Wilson notes that Trump *did* campaign on an authoritarian platform in 2024, threatening to use his powers in office, including declaring a national emergency over immigration (Hutzler,

2024) and taking revenge both on those who betrayed him and 'the enemies from within' (Cooper, 2024).

Meanwhile, Trump's attacks on the media have continued, whilst the Republicans, and Vance especially, have spent the last few years targeting universities. Previously, Yarvin coined the (deliberately-chosen) acronym 'RAGE', which stood for the plan he wanted to see implemented of 'Retire All Government Employees', in order to dismantle the deep-state functionaries of the Cathedral (Michael, 2022). Elon Musk's DOGE seems tasked with a similar stripping of employees. The exit from democracy, therefore, may already be well-advanced.

And if that does happen, then that authoritarian rule will initially be celebrated by Trump's supporters and by a public who want to see that political system punished for its faithlessness, for its abandonment of them, for its divorce from their everyday lives and concerns. They will happily misinterpret elite *exit* as populist *re-entry*. They will see the Trumpian deconstruction of that system of 'democracy' as a joyful thing and a new beginning—the start of a new relationship to the government and a reinvestment of it in their cares and concerns—a hope that is unlikely to be fulfilled.

Unless?

Unless the tensions in Trump's coalition become too much. Could the different anti-democratic trajectories of Trumpian voters—exit and re-entry—split his support? Could the tension between the neo-liberal elite with their tax-cuts and deregulation and the anti-neo-liberal people wishing for the reappearance of meaningful jobs and lives and communities become too obvious? Could the tension between the elite, Randian faith in creative destruction jar too much with a nativist populism whose vision looks to the past rather than the future? Could the appeal of disruption be limited by those who've already had decades of neo-liberal disruption? Could the cos-play of Trumpian patriotism be sufficient to keep his core voters happy? If no real change can happen for them on the ground, then could Trump still buy off their hopes with an endless parade of enemies and revenge, with his TV-show performance, with his rallies and with his effortless incitement of hatred and anger and release of laughter. All of which pushes the real question: can he continue to appropriate and channel their rage, or will it, one day, turn against him?

# CHAPTER 6

# Conclusion: *Zombie Capitalism* and the Rage of the Undead

**Abstract** This chapter maps the rise of 'zombie capitalism', arguing that the 2008 financial crash ushered in a period of unending neo-liberal austerity, creating a system akin to the undead—persisting despite its internal decay and societal damage. The zombie is not just a horror figure but a symbol of the decaying and unthinking systems that dominate our lives. We conclude that unless we can reverse the epistemic sharding of experiences and metastatisation of the real by the digital self and reestablish shared worlds, relations, concepts and solutions, then our realities will remain radically separate, fractalised and digitally kaleidoscopic.

**Keywords** Zombie capitalism · De-socialism · Media · Society of the selfie

> There'll be the breaking of the ancient Western code
> Your private life will suddenly explode
> There'll be phantoms
> There'll be fires on the road
> And the white man dancing
> ...I've seen the future, baby it is murder

Leonard Cohen 'The Future' (1992)

The 'zombie' has become, perhaps, *the* quintessential figure of modern horror. Zombies originated in Haitian folklore, within the Voodoo culture and belief system, as re-animated figures of the dead, before the concept spread to the west. They appeared in early US horror films, including *White Zombie* (1932) and *I Walked With a Zombie* (1943), but it was George A. Romero's 1968 film *Night of the Living Dead* and its sequels that transformed them into a cult phenomenon. For a long time, however, they remained low down the 'monster' rank, making only occasional appearances in the horror tradition. That began to change from the mid-1990s, with their appearance in new films and video-games until, by the early 2000s, they were experiencing a remarkable renaissance, spreading throughout popular culture. Arguably, it was *The Walking Dead* comic (2003–2019) and television series (2010–2022) that did most to reanimate their popular appeal.

That appeal is complex, because unlike other classic horror monsters it's not just about them, as zombies are connected to, and are often the products of, some kind of mass-societal event. In *Night of the Living Dead*, the mass-reanimation was itself the event, but almost all subsequent representations blame some kind of mass-catastrophe such as a plague or virus for their creation and for the apocalyptic end of civilisation. Indeed, it is this end of civilisation, as much as the zombies, that is at the heart of the horror and fascination. All of this, therefore, represents a significant development beyond the Haitian model, which had been focused on religious practices and the dead individual. What had also changed was their behaviour, with the zombie stereotyped now as an ever-advancing, decaying mass, driven by hunger and unthinking rage.

Perhaps it's no coincidence that their contemporary appeal aligns with our own mass-catastrophe event: that of the ravages of late global neo-liberalism, its 2008 crash and its aftermath. Just as 1973's recession represented the symbolic moment of breakdown of the post-war Keynesian welfare state, so the 2008 crash represents the same for the neo-liberal state system that emerged to replace it. Except, in 1973 the search for the new took only a few years, with early monetarist solutions being introduced before the rise of the new right at the end of the decade. In contrast, 2008 represented the moment of our entry into an unending, post-apocalyptic wasteland—we have had over a decade and a half since the crash with nothing new appearing. Indeed, not only have we had no new economic orientation, we have had *more and more neo-liberalism*, especially in the unending 'austerity' introduced to solve the very problem of neo-liberalism.

So this is where we are now, left with an undead, *zombie capitalism*: one continuing to survive, but condemned to stumble on without any new thought or self-understanding; unhealthy, rotting away, reduced almost to its bones and feeding on the surviving human populations, driven by it's a rage at their needs, their resistant life and the public services and welfare benefits they demand. There is, of course, a history of zombies as a critique of capitalism. Romero's 1978 *Dawn of the Dead* had the zombies wandering around a shopping mall looking like consumers— leading to the key line, 'They are us!'—whilst, afterwards, the heroes use the mall's goods for themselves, enabling them to pleasurably escape from the reality outside (Gregory, 2024). Now that catastrophe is global.

And the system simply goes on, dedicated to its programming—to the rejection of the redistributive state and the promotion of infinite austerity, cutting away forever, shambling forward under the momentum of its own undead philosophy and system. But it isn't only a zombie economics that we have—there is the zombie political system that supports it too. The 2016 earthquake of Brexit in the UK and Trump in the US was, more than anything else, a message to mainstream politics and politicians. It was a warning that something they thought was working fine had become damagingly disconnected from the lives, problems, desires and demands of many of the electorate.

In the UK, the initial zombie response of the incoming 2010 conservative/ liberal-democratic government to the crash was a turbocharged neo-liberalism with a radical austerity programme to slash public spending even further. David Cameron's political project, however, would be derailed by Brexit and by the public and party turn towards populism that would lead, by 2019, to the premiership of Boris Johnson. The Tories subsequent infighting, political decline and failure in the 2024 election, was seen by some as a return to centrist normality. Labour supporters were jubilant at what looked like a significant, era-defining reversal, with 411 seats and a majority of 174, but that would prove to be a serious misreading of what had just happened. Because the Tory vote crumbled not just because people turned to a left alternative, in the Liberal Democrats, the Green party and Labour, but because they (as well as Labour) haemorrhaged votes to the angry, populist right.

The real story of the 2024 UK election was the 5 seats Reform won. They won 5 because of the first-past-the-post electoral system, but their sudden rise to 4.1m votes compared worryingly well to the Conservative's 6.8m and Labour's 9.7m. From almost nowhere they had risen to stand against the mainstream parties. Indeed, in many seats they became the second-placed party, poised for the next electoral contest, Watching on X and TikTok the flood of pro-Reform material and the overtly-racist, hate-filled, incendiary, rage-fuelled comments, posts and videos in the time leading up to and after the election, it was clear that this would lead to violence. That violence took less than a month to materialise and it has remained since, simmering in the background. Very simply, Reform are going to become one of the most important and powerful voices in UK politics (perhaps *the* most), and, as the continuing digital posts saying, 'enough is enough', calling for 'mobilisation' and for British people to 'fight' suggest, the nativist, racism of their supporters will almost certainly lead to more violence.

In the US, it seemed for many Democrat supporters that common sense had returned in 2020 and that a centrist faith in political normality and the democratic system had been reestablished. Given that, there was obviously no need to change anything, or to learn the lesson of the Trump interregnum. All that people wanted, it was assumed, was business-again-as-normal after the convulsions of Trump, of Covid-19, of the protests and violence and of the failed insurrection. This was also a significant misreading of the political situation and its volatility. The Democrat's zombie-like option of stumbling on without a moment's thought would prove an error. Trump's return would show that there hadn't been a blip, now cured by the Democrats, but rather that a real problem remained and it couldn't be ignored any longer. If sharded realities aided the populist insurgency in the UK and US, the mainstream parties have been left trapped and damaged by their own sharding. And, like in Britain, as the shooting of the UnitedHealth CEO shows, the problem of the US public's rage and their propensity to violence also remains very real.

In 1989 Francis Fukuyama famously hailed the victory of liberal political and economic systems as 'the end of history' (Fukuyama, 1989). Jean Baudrillard, as always, was more interesting. 'Prophesying catastrophe is incredibly banal', he said. 'The more original move is to assume it has already occurred. This changes all the conditions of analysis' (Baudrillard, 1996a: 68–69). The real question, therefore, is what does it mean to live on *after the end*. This is where we are. What does it mean to live on today, under zombie capitalism and zombie liberal democracy?

In one scenario, we simply remain zombies within this zombie system. It all carries on and nothing changes, with the continuing hollowing out of life and society, the infinite cutting of services and the perpetual rotting of experiences. This is the endless neo-liberal enshittification of the real. The 'socialism' Von Mises and Hayek hated so much led, with the eventual victory of neo-liberalism in the west, to a deliberate, systematic process of *de-socialism*: an attack on welfare-capitalism and the rights of the working man and on the roots of socialism—the very *existence* of the working class itself and their industries and lives. Global neo-liberalism deliberately de-industrialised the west, destroying the economic basis of working-class life and resistance. Hence, the second, interlinked impact of neo-liberalism: a deliberate, systematic *de-social-ism*: the destruction not just of working-class communities, but of community itself, of the connective social tissue of place, habitation, stability, personal memory and generational history and its culture, leaving only the voidal realities of post-industrial, post-zombie-apocalypse wastelands, with entire regions left behind by the globalised dream, home to satellised towns, cheap shops and lonely, disconnected and physically and mentally vulnerable populations, often addicted to gambling, anti-depressants or opioids like fentanyl (see Mind, 2024; Yousif, 2023).

And in its place, as *the replacement social*, we got, as Richard Hoggart foresaw so long ago (Hoggart, 2009), the brash world of global consumerism, with television, popular mass-culture and, with the digital revolution, smartphones and social media, all now created by and sold for the profit of the great, beneficent, neo-liberal tech-giants of today. Apple, Meta, Alphabet, X: their neo-liberal businesses are all built on technologies of separation and simulation, all to replace the relationships and meaning that neo-liberalism itself voided so long ago. This is a world of sharded, personalised *me*-dia experiences, bringing populations together virtually, within the hierophanic blue-light of the screen that today irradiates all our politics, our mental health, our relationships, our children and human sleep itself. Their AI algorithms 'feed' us, bringing us the content that forms our world and *reality-diet*, the promotion of 'engagement' leading to a preference for stickiness, for outrage, for dopamine-hits, all of which propels us forward forever, fixed to our phones, hungry for more hits, more likes, more emoji-reactions, whilst filled with an empty, dead-eyed fury. We are all the rage-filled undead of Western neo-liberalism.

De-socialism and de-social-ism: *exit* and *sharding*. What are the hopes, therefore, of reversal? What are the hopes of re-entry and re-connection?

In power, the options taken by the centrist Democratic Party in the US and Labour Party in the UK have been insufficient, seeking only the better management of neo-liberalism, remaining bound to its infinite concept of 'growth' and to the markets, trying to reinject the social in homeopathic amounts, whilst apologising for the economic realities of the system and managing financial expectations. This isn't enough. What the public want is a much more serious re-entry—a sustained and efficacious reinjection of government concern and care. Whilst ever they remain impoverished, with their lives ruled by precarity and fear, they will remain defensive, resentful, reactionary, open to the appeals of the populist right and potentially violent. When people are doing better and are more secure and happy in their own condition and status, they are less likely to look around and punch down at perceived threats.

What are people looking for from their government? Their current anti-liberalism actually provides a clue. Their anger at the government is anger at a system that has failed to live up to its Lockean promises of supporting the rights of the people and of ensuring their protection. They want re-entry: theirs is a demand for recognition by the state, for the recognition of their humanity and the fulfilment of what remain, at heart, very basic hopes: they want good health, good education, they want that education to be rewarded, they want jobs that won't kill them and will support them, they want families, they want housing, food and energy they can afford, and they want infrastructure, services and systems around them that are not failing or rotting. They want a state that looks over them and puts their lives, needs and concerns first and that reinvests in and protects the social. They want an alternative to the remote politics of the political system and the worship of global neo-liberalism. The chances of this re-entry happening appear slim. Continued orbitalised government and left-behind rage and sporadic violence are more probable.

What about sharding? What hope is there of liberal re-connection, the reinstitution of shared worlds and promotion of democratic, rational-critical political debate and compromise? The liberal state has largely failed to curb the excesses of media technology over the last 30 years. The US government, especially, has deliberately promoted a neo-liberal, laisser-faire approach, promoting platform indemnity (Kosseff, 2019) and refusing regulation (Bradford, 2023; Schaake, 2024), though recent years have seen more interest in questioning technology-company power. Europe has shown more desire to regulate, introducing strong protections on certain issues such as privacy, through the GDPR. It is only now, however, that they are trying to mitigate the worst harms of these platforms and their content through, for example, the EU Digital Services Act 2022 and Artificial Intelligence (AI) Act 2024 and the UK Online Safety Act 2023. Their ability, however, to stop the flood of online material, to prevent access to it and to keep up with technologies and popular uses that have already potentially made the acts redundant means that optimism here is difficult to sustain.

The fact that, two US elections on from 2016, liberals and academics are still obsessed with disinformation and how to combat it, exposes how out-of-touch their shard of reality is. For many, there is still the belief that if only we could fact-check and point out the 'truth' then we could defeat fake news and stop its harms. What this misses is that it is people who are deliberately creating it and they are doing so because they and others *want* it. As Stephen Colbert understood way back in 2005, 'truthiness'—the intuitive feeling that something is still true, even if it may not be—is more important than 'truth' (Zimmer, 2010). We *like* information that agrees with us and our politics, and so those most receptive to it are least likely to accept fact-checking by self-proclaimed, 'mainstream' authorities. But fact-checking keeps the liberal/left happy, as they devote all their energies to their own rage—*a rage at the lying of the right*— a rage, to their endless confusion and consternation, simply not shared by everyone else. Meanwhile, the anti-liberal-progressivism of the culture wars will continue online unabated, as a highly-emotional and enjoyable, participative game, open to all sides, who can pursue their own informational wars against whatever evil they identify, all using the profitable technologies, platforms and services of the neo-liberal elite.

We are right to worry about the effects of sharding on democracy, but not so much because of disinformation or culture wars and cancellation, but because of the structural transformation of communication wrought by digital technology. Because democracy is about *others*: it's fundamentally about accepting that others exist, that they have a right to their opinions, that we'll get the chance to share our opinions, make a decision collectively about what we want for all of us, and accept the result together and compromise. Digital *me*-dia, however, is not about others, it is *about me*: it constitutes a Ptolemaic revolution in which the universe now revolves around the individual, as they produce, share, collect and curate their own real. Guy Debord wrote in 1967 about the mass-media 'society of the spectacle', an idea Baudrillard would extend in the digital age where, he argued, 'We are no longer spectators but actors in the performance' (Baudrillard, 1996b: 27), but even he couldn't anticipate the reversal that placed the performative-self as central to all reality. This is no longer the society of the spectacle: it is *the society of the selfie*. In a detournement of Debord, we might suggest that 'The spectacle *really is* a collection of images...A social relation with ourselves, mediated by images of ourselves'.

Consider 'Princess Breanna's' 2014 tweet, 'Selfie in the Auschwitz Concentration Camp' (Zarrell, 2014). Her smiling face fills the image, pushing the actual buildings and their historical reality out of the scene. To paraphrase Baudrillard's famous critique of the 1991 Gulf War, the Holocaust here cannot take (a) place—pushed out by the self's grinning, photographic evidence of its own presence; its final, definitive, undeniable historical proof *of itself*; that *it* was there and *its visit* happened. Hence our new, more dangerous form of denialism: not the exculpatory denialism of Holocaust revisionists desperate to disprove the event, but the replacement of the historical event and its reality with *ourselves* and our experiences and feelings. If, for Adorno, to write poetry after Auschwitz was barbaric, what would he say of Princess Breanna's Auschwitz happy-face emoji?

Or consider the film of *The Lord of the Rings*. There, the fellowship pause for a while on their quest, taking refuge in the eleven kingdom of Lothlórien, meeting the Lady Galadriel. At a crucial moment, when offered the ring of power, she senses a possibility, suddenly rising up before us as a terrifying, spectral god, announcing, 'In place of a Dark Lord, you would have a queen! Not dark, but beautiful and terrible as the dawn! Treacherous as the sea! Stronger than the foundations of the earth! All shall love me, and despair!' (TheLotrTV, 2013). In the age of the self-papparised, hyporeal self, we are all Galadriel: today, the digital self rises, beautiful and terrible, demanding that *all shall click heart and despair*.

This is the new, digital categorical imperative of self-communication: the self *must produce*, it must continuously return to record itself again, to respond and update itself, globally broadcasting our posed and composed, edited and filtered selves. Berkeley's *esse est percipi*—to be is to be perceived—offers now not a transcendental but a terrestrial, semiotic reassurance, for our existence must be recognised and confirmed by our networks, by the quantities of followers and notifications. The post without engagement is a dead moment that strikes to the core of the self. Whereas Nietzsche's 'will-to-power' was a positive force, an internal mode of self-creation and overcoming, we are locked instead into *the will-to-selfie*: an opposing force representing the declination of life and its replacement with its curated, outward-facing simulacra. Instead of a procreative will of life, we spend our time *not living*, refining the image of life, in a self-slavery without end, producing 100 selfies for each one we use, and eternally, obsessively, returning to our feeds. The 1960s radical slogan, 'the personal is political', designed to show how everyday experience was politically structured, reverses now into *politics is the personal*: an identitarian, self-centred creed that no longer opposes the system but is the perfect reflection of neo-liberal individualism.

Hence the society of the selfie, the society of me-dia, of happy-faced emojis, of self-paparizzization, of the panic-stricken production of the self, of the furious spectral god demanding love, of the pornographic exposure of the self, of the obscene digital loquacity of the stream of personal opinions, thoughts, invective and commentary—all of this is structurally anti-democratic. Like the blocks of Auschwitz, the systems of democracy and the others who populate it are all pushed aside in favour of our own grinning selves. The sharding of media and of the real is metastasised by the digital self. And if we and our opinions are indeed so important, then why should we listen to others, or compromise with them? Their difference is instead today an assault we need protecting from. With the block button creating 'safe' spaces for us, free from 'hate', we can now fight the whole world, or cancel it if we wish. But a media world structured around *my self* and *my rage* leaves little room for the other, and, by definition, for democracy.

Unless we can reverse the epistemic sharding of experiences and metastatisation of the real by the digital self and reestablish shared worlds, relations, concepts and solutions, then our realities will remain radically separate, fractalised and digitally kaleidoscopic. Perhaps a government dedicated to re-entry, to putting the actual needs of the public first, to reigning in the worst aspects of the digital revolution and to reconnecting the public could make an attempt to achieve this. But that would take a very different kind of politics, and a very different politician to the one that was inaugurated on 20th January 2025.

# Bibliography

Adragna, A. (2024, November 6). Bernie Sanders Blasts Democratic Party Following Harris Loss. *Politico*. https://www.politico.com/live-updates/2024/11/06/2024-election-results-live-coverage-updates-analysis/bernie-sanders-election-response-00187980

Al Jazeera. (2022, October 28). Saudis 'Second Largest Investors' in Twitter After Musk takeover'. *Al Jazeera*. https://www.aljazeera.com/news/2022/10/28/saudis-kingdom-holding-company-to-maintain-twitter-stake

Anderson, B. (2016). *Imagined Communities*. Verso.

Anderson, C. (2006). *The Long Tail*. Random House Business Books.

Andreessen, M. (2023, October 16). The Techno-Optimist Manifesto. *Andreessen-Horowitz*. https://a16z.com/the-techno-optimist-manifesto/

Anonymous. (2019). *A Warning*. London: Little, Brown Book Group.

Badham, V. (2022). *QAnon and On*. Hardie Grant Books.

Baldwin, T. (2018). *Ctrl Alt Del: How Politics and the Media Crashed Our Democracy*. C. Hurst and Co.

Ball, J. (2018). *Post-Truth*. Biteback Publishing.

Ball, J. (2023). *The Other Pandemic: How QAnon Contaminated the World*. Bloomsbury Publishing.

Bancroft, H. (2024, October 24). Cost of Housing an Asylum Seeker 'Soars from £17k to £41k in Just Four Years' as Hotel Use Surges'. *The Independent*. https://www.independent.co.uk/news/uk/home-news/migrant-asylum-seeker-home-office-housing-hotel-b2634213.html

Barbrook, R., & Cameron, A. (1995, September 1). The Californian Ideology. *Mute Magazine*. https://www.metamute.org/editorial/articles/californian-ideology

Barlow, J. P. (1996, February 8). A Declaration of Independence of Cyberspace. *Electronic Frontier Foundation*. https://www.eff.org/cyberspace-independence

Barr, J. (2024, December 25). At CNN, Lower TV Ratings and Heightened Anxieties About What's Ahead. *The Washington Post*. https://www.washingtonpost.com/style/media/2024/12/25/cnn-ratings-decline-trump/

Barthes, R. (1993). *Camera Lucida*. Vintage.

Baudrillard, J. (1987). *Forget Foucault*. Semiotext(e).

Baudrillard, J. (1988). *America*. Verso.

Baudrillard, J. (1990a). *Fatal Strategies*. Semiotext(e).

Baudrillard, J. (1990b). *Seduction*. New World Perspectives.

Baudrillard, J. (1996a). *Cool Memories II*. Polity Press.

Baudrillard, J. (1996b). *The Perfect Crime*. Verso.

Baudrillard, J. (1998). *The Consumer Society*. Sage.

Baudrillard, J. (2005). *The Intelligence of Evil or the Lucidity Pact*. Berg.

BBC. (2015, November 26). Donald Trump under Fire for Mocking Disabled Reporter. *BBC News*. https://www.bbc.co.uk/news/world-us-canada-34930042

BBC. (2016a, April 15). Reality Check: Would Brexit Mean Extra £350m a Week for NHS? *BBC News*. https://www.bbc.co.uk/news/uk-politics-eu-referendum-36040060

BBC. (2016b, June 8). Turkey EU Accession Poses Security Risk—Michael Gove. *BBC News*. https://www.bbc.co.uk/news/uk-politics-eu-referendum-36479259

BBC. (2017a, February 18). Is Donald Trump Good for Journalism? *The Inquiry*, BBC World Service, first broadcast. http://www.bbc.co.uk/programmes/p04s45sg

BBC. (2017b, June 22). 'Pizzagate' Gunman Sentenced to Four Years. *BBC News*. https://www.bbc.co.uk/news/world-us-canada-40372407

BBC. (2017c, October 1). Trump to Tillerson: N Korea Negotiations a Waste of Time. *BBC News*. https://www.bbc.co.uk/news/world-us-canada-41460205

BBC. (2018, October 24). 'Explosive Devices' Sent to Clinton, Obama, CNN, and Other US Officials. *BBC News*. https://www.bbc.co.uk/news/world-us-canada-45969100

BBC. (2020a, April 24). Coronavirus: Outcry After Trump Suggests Injecting Disinfectant as Treatment. *BBC News*. https://www.bbc.co.uk/news/world-us-canada-52407177

BBC. (2020b, June 24). President Trump Calls Coronavirus "Kung Flu". *BBC News*. https://www.bbc.co.uk/news/av/world-us-canada-53173436

BBC. (2020c, October 29). US Election 2020: Trump Slams Lockdowns, Biden Accuses Him of Insulting Victims. *BBC News*. https://www.bbc.co.uk/news/election-us-2020-54727919

BBC. (2021a). Anglesey Kidnap: Gang Jailed for Snatching Child over Satanic Abuse Fears. *BBC News.* https://www.bbc.co.uk/news/uk-wales-58753545

BBC. (2021b, January 27). Covid: Wrexham Vaccine Production Resumes After Suspect Package. *BBC News.* https://www.bbc.co.uk/news/uk-wales-55822838

BBC. (2023, August 3). Bud Light Boycott over Trans Influencer Dylan Mulvaney Hits Beer Giant's Sales. *BBC News.* https://www.bbc.co.uk/news/business-66398296

BBC. (2024a, November 15). *Today.* BBC Radio 4.

BBC. (2024b, November 7). Five Reasons Why Kamala Harris Lose to Donald Trump. *BBC News.* https://www.bbc.com/pidgin/articles/c5yr2nen09xo

BBC. (2024c, November 7). Why Kamala Harris Lost: A Flawed Candidate or Doomed Campaign? *BBC News.* https://www.bbc.co.uk/news/articles/cjr4l5j2v9do

Beckett, A. (2017, May 11). Accelerationism: How a Fringe Philosophy Predicted the Future We Live In. *The Guardian.* https://www.theguardian.com/world/2017/may/11/accelerationism-how-a-fringe-philosophy-predicted-the-future-we-live-in

Benkler, Y. (2006). *The Wealth of Networks.* Yale University Press.

Benkler, Y., Faris, R., Roberts, H., & Zuckerman, E. (2017, March 3). Study: Breitbart-led Right-Wing Ecosystem Altered Broader Media Aganda. *Columbia Journalism Review.* https://www.cjr.org/analysis/breitbart-media-trump-harvard-study.php

Binkley, C. (2024, January 13). As a New Generation Rises, Tension Between Free Speech and Inclusivity on College Campuses Simmers. *AP News.* https://apnews.com/article/campus-free-speech-young-generation-tension-b931b0dd41aacaac5c50710de9549b09

Bloom, M., & Moskalenko, S. (2021). *Pastels and Pedophiles. Inside the Mind of QAnon.* Redwood Press.

Bokhari, A. (2017, March 4). Study: Breitbart Dominated Right Wing Coverage, 'Altered Media Agenda' in 2016. https://www.breitbart.com/tech/2017/03/04/study-breitbart-led-right-wing-media-ecosystem-altered-media-agenda/

Boorstin, D. J. (1992). *[1961]).* Vintage Books.

Bond, S. (2023, June 13). AI-generated Images Are Everywhere. Here's How to Spot Them. *NPR.* https://www.npr.org/2023/06/07/1180768459/how-to-identify-ai-generated-deepfake-images

Boyer, D. (2007). *Understanding Media: A Popular Philosophy.* Prickly Paradigm.

Bradford, A. (2023). *Digital Empires.* Oxford University Press.

Bradner, E. (2017, January 23). Conway: Trump White House Offered 'Alternative Facts' on Crowd Size. *CNN.* https://edition.cnn.com/2017/01/22/politics/kellyanne-conway-alternative-facts/index.html

Brenton, H. (2021, May 1). Italian Police Arrest Two Anti-vaxxers for Fire-Bombing of Vaccination Hub. *Politico*. https://www.politico.eu/article/italy-police-arrest-coronavirus-vaccination-hub-bomb-brescia/

Bridges, T. (2017, February 27). Why People Are So Averse to Facts. *The Society Pages*. https://thesocietypages.org/socimages/2017/02/27/why-the-american-public-seems-allergic-to-facts/

Bugliosi, V. (2018). *Helter Skelter*. Penguin Books.

Burrows, R. (2018, September 29). On Neoreaction and Other Romantic Delusions. *The Sociological Review*. https://thesociologicalreview.org/projects/undisciplining/talks-discussions-and-debates/on-neoreaction/

Burton, L. (2024, November 7). Guardian Offers Therapy to Staff After 'Devastating' Trump Election Win. *The Telegraph*. https://www.telegraph.co.uk/business/2024/11/07/guardian-offers-staff-counselling-after-trump-win/

Cadwalladr, C. (2024a, November 10). A New Era Dawns. America's Tech Bros Now Strut Their Stuff in the Corridors of Power. *The Observer*. https://www.theguardian.com/commentisfree/2024/nov/11/a-new-era-dawns-americas-tech-bros-now-strut-their-stuff-in-the-corridors-of-power

Cadwalladr, C. (2024b, November 10). Fight the Power. And Other Hard Things. Join Me. *Substack*. https://broligarchy.substack.com/p/fight-the-power

Cadwalladr, C. (2024c, November 17). How to Survive the Broligarchy: 20 Lessons for the Post-Truth World. *The Guardian*. https://www.theguardian.com/commentisfree/2024/nov/17/how-to-survive-the-broligarchy-20-lessons-for-the-post-truth-world-donald-trump

Callinicos, A. (1989). *Against Postmodernism. A Marxist Critique*. Polity Press.

Camus, R. (2018). *You Will Not Replace Us!* Chez l'auteur, 32340 Plieux.

Camus, R. (2024). *The Great Replacement: Introduction to Global Replacism*. Editions du Chateau, Plieux.

Caramanica, J. (2024, November 14). Where to Find the Avuncular Donald Trump? Check the Manosphere. *The New York Times*. https://www.nytimes.com/2024/11/14/arts/donald-trump-podcasts-men.html

Cavendish, S., MacFarquhar, N., McGee, J., & Goldman, A. (2021, February 24). Behind the Nashville Bombing, a Conspiracy Theorist Stewing About the Government. *New York Times*. https://www.nytimes.com/2021/02/24/us/anthony-warner-nashville-bombing.html

CCRU. (2017). *Writings 1997–2003: (Urbanomic) by Cybernetic Culture Research Unit (CCRU)*. Urbanomic Media Ltd.

Cecco, L. (2020, July 3). Armed Man Roamed Justin Trudeau's Grounds for 13 Minutes After Ramming Gates. *The Guardian*. https://www.theguardian.com/world/2020/jul/03/armed-man-roamed-justin-trudeaus-grounds-for-13-minutes-after-ramming-gates

Chafkin, M. (2022). *The Contrarian*. Bloomsbury Publishing.

Chantler Hicks, L. (2022, November 25). Elon Musk Says He's "Not Right Wing" but "Woke Mind Virus Pushing Civilisation Toward Suicide". *The Standard.* https://www.standard.co.uk/news/world/twitter-elon-musk-woke-mind-virus-tesla-b1042726.html

Chapman, L., Wagner, K., & TNS. (2022, February 6). Peter Thiel to Leave Meta Board to Pursue Trump Political Agenda. *The Jerusalem Post.* https://www.jpost.com/business-and-innovation/article-695874

Christian, B. (2019, October 22). Donald Trump Accused of Flicking Middle Finger at Female Astronauts During Video Call with International Space Station. *The Standard.* https://www.standard.co.uk/news/world/trump-flips-middle-finger-at-astronauts-during-video-call-with-iss-a4267671.html

Clayton, F. (2024, November 25). Elon Musk Brands Britain a 'Tyrannical Police State' and Boosts Far-right Activist. *NBC News.* https://www.nbcnews.com/news/world/elon-musk-britain-police-state-starmer-election-tommy-robinson-rcna181593

Clinton, H. (2010, January 21). Remarks on Internet Freedom. *U.S. Department of State.* https://2009-2017.state.gov/secretary/20092013clinton/rm/2010/01/135519.htm

Clinton, H. (2011). Remarks at the OSCE First Plenary Session. LitExpo Conference Center, Vilnius, Lithuania, December 6, *U.S. Department of State.* https://2009-2017.state.gov/secretary/20092013clinton/rm/2011/12/178315.htm

Cole, B. (2024, December 21). Magdeburg Attack Suspect Said Elon Musk, Alex Jones 'Telling Truth': Report. *Newsweek.* https://www.newsweek.com/germany-magdeburg-terrorism-musk-2004573

Coleman, A. (2021, March 6). Covid Lockdown: Why Magna Carta Won't Exempt You from the Rules. *BBC News.* https://www.bbc.co.uk/news/56295261

Connolly, K. (2024, December 20). Outrage as Elon Musk Claims "Only AfD Can Save Germany". *The Guardian.* https://www.theguardian.com/world/2024/dec/20/elon-musk-claims-only-afd-can-save-germany

Cooper, J. J. (2024, October 26). Who Does Trump See as "Enemies from Within"?' *AP.* https://apnews.com/article/donald-trump-enemies-from-within-5c4a34776469a55e71d3ba4d4e68cf62

Corbin, I. M. (2024, July 24). What's Behind America's Loneliness Crisis? *Commonweal.* https://www.commonwealmagazine.org/whats-behind-americas-loneliness-crisis

Cotterill, T., & Tozer, J. (2024, November 13). Moment Public Meeting Descends into Chaos as Locals Are Told Hotel Migrants 'Will Be Given Private Healthcare' to Stop Them Being a Burden on 'Very Stretched' Services'. *Daily Mail.* https://www.dailymail.co.uk/news/article-14077423/moment-residents-told-migrants-altrincham-receive-private-healthcare.html

D'Ancona, M. (2017). *Post-Truth*. Ebury Press.

Davis, E. (1998). *Techgnosis: Myth, Magic, and Mysticism in the Age of Information*. Serpent's Tail.

Davis, E. (2017). *Post-Truth*. Little, Brown.

Davidson, J. D., & Rees-Mogg, W. (2020). *The Sovereign Individual*. Simon and Schuster.

Dayan, D. (2013, February 24). Overhearing in the Public Sphere. *Deliberately Considered*. http://www.deliberatelyconsidered.com/2013/02/overhearing-in-the-public-sphere/

Dearden, L. (2020, September 1). 'New Forms of Terrorism Inspired by Conspiracy Theories May Emerge After Pandemic, Warns EU Counter-Terror Chief'. *The Independent*. https://www.independent.co.uk/news/uk/home-news/coronavirus-conspiracy-theory-terrorism-5g-gilles-de-kerchove-a9699571.html

Debord, G. (1977). *Society of the Spectacle*. Black & Red. https://www.marxists.org/reference/archive/debord/society.htm

Debusmann, B., Jr. (2023, June 29). Affirmative Action: US Supreme Court Overturns Race-Based College Admissions. *BBC News*. https://www.bbc.co.uk/news/world-us-canada-65886212

Deibert, R. J. (2013). *Black Code*. McClelland and Stewart.

Deneen, P. J. (2018). *Why Liberalism Failed*. Yale University Press.

Devlin, K., & Cheetham, J. (2023, March 24). Fake Trump Arrest Photos: How to Spot an AI-generated Image. https://www.bbc.co.uk/news/world-us-canada-65069316

Doctorow, C. (2023, January 23). The "Enshittification" of TikTok, or How, Exactly, Platforms Die. *Wired*. https://www.wired.com/story/tiktok-platforms-cory-doctorow/

Dorling, D. (2015). *Inequality and the 1%*. Verso.

Dorn, S. (2022, November 27). Elon Musk's Political Shift: How the Billionaire Moved from Backing Obama to Endorsing DeSantis. *Forbes*. https://www.forbes.com/sites/saradorn/2022/11/27/elon-musks-political-shift-how-the-billionaire-moved-from-backing-obama-to-endorsing-desantis/

Duggan, L. (2019). *Mean Girl*. University of California Press.

Eatwell, R., & Goodwin, M. (2018). *National Populism: The Revolt Against Liberal Democracy*. Pelican.

EHA. (2024). Immigration to the United States. *Economic History Association*. https://eh.net/encyclopedia/immigration-to-the-united-states/#:~:text=For%20the%20period%20from%201847,the%20United%20States%20each%20year

Epstein, R. J., Lerer, L., & Nehamas, N. (2024, November 7). Devastated Democrats Play the Blame Game, and Stare at a Dark Future. *New York*

*Times.* https://www.nytimes.com/2024/11/07/us/politics/democrats-kam ala-harris.html

Faguy, A., & FitzGerald, J. (2024, November 13). Donald Trump Picks Elon Musk for New Cost-Cutting Role. *BBC News.* https://www.bbc.co.uk/ news/articles/c93qwn8p0l0o

Fahrenthold, D. A. (2016, October 8). Trump Recorded Having Extremely Lewd Conversation About Women in 2005. *The Washington Post.* https:// www.washingtonpost.com/politics/trump-recorded-having-extremely-lewd-conversation-about-women-in-2005/2016/10/07/3b9ce776-8cb4-11e6-bf8a-3d26847eeed4_story.html

Fanon, F. (2021). *Black Skin, White Masks.* Penguin.

Farrell, H. (2024). No Exit Opportunities: Business Models and Political Thought in Silicon Valley. *American Affairs Journal, VIII*(3), 195–208.

Feinberg, A. (2023, April 18). Trump Lashes Out at Elon Musk after Tech Mogul Says He Voted for Biden. *The Independent.* https://www.the-indepe ndent.com/news/world/americas/us-politics/donald-trump-elon-musk-tuc ker-carlson-b2322101.html

Francis, S., & Eardley, N. (2023, September 19). Migrant Hotel Costs Rise to £8m a Day, Home Office Figures Show. *BBC News.* https://www.bbc.co.uk/ news/uk-politics-66855830

Freedland, J. (2017, April 10). The New Age of Ayn Rand: How She Won over Trump and Silicon Valley. *The Guardian.* https://www.theguardian.com/ books/2017/apr/10/new-age-ayn-rand-conquered-trump-white-house-sil icon-valley

Frenkel, S., & Isaac, M. (2024, September 24). How Meta Distanced Itself From Politics. *The New York Times.* https://www.nytimes.com/2024/09/24/tec hnology/meta-election-politics.html

Friedan, B. (2010). *The Feminine Mystique.* Penguin.

Fukuyama, F. (1989). The End of History? *The National Interest*, No. 16, Summer, pp. 3–18.

Fuller, S. (2018). *Post-Truth.* Anthem Press.

Gabbatt, A. (2021, February 1). Claim of Anti-conservative Bias by Social Media Firms Is Baseless, Report Finds. *The Guardian.* https://www.thegua rdian.com/media/2021/feb/01/facebook-youtube-twitter-anti-conservative-claims-baseless-report-finds

Gabbatt, A. (2023, September 19). 'Subtle and Sinister': Republicans' Anti-drag Crusade Seen as Assault on LGBTQ+ Rights. *The Guardian.* https://www. theguardian.com/world/2023/sep/19/us-states-attack-drag-shows-lgbtq-rights

Gabbatt, A. (2024, December 16). The Right Believes the Healthcare CEO Shooting Suspect Is a 'Liberal Wacko'. The Truth Is Complicated.

*The Guardian.* https://www.theguardian.com/us-news/2024/dec/16/uni
tedhealthcare-suspect-political-beliefs

Galtung, J., & Ruge, M. H. (1965). The Structure of Foreign News: The Presentation of the Congo, Cuba and Cyprus Crises in Four Norwegian Newspapers.
*Journal of Peace Research, 2*(1), 64–90. https://doi.org/10.1177/002234
336500200104

Gamble, A. (1989). *The Free Economy and the Strong State.* Macmillan Education
Ltd.

Gitlin, T. (1980). *The Whole World is Watching—Mass Media in the Making and
Unmaking of the New Left.* University of California Press.

Gecker, J., & Lurye, S. (2024, November 13). Trump Made Anti-trans
Themes Key to His Campaign. Transgender teenagers are scared. *The
Independent.* https://www.independent.co.uk/news/world/americas/us-pol
itics/donald-trump-transgender-teenagers-school-b2646561.html

Gerken, T. (2024a, March 25). Elon Musk's X Anti-hate Group Case Thrown
Out. *BBC News.* https://www.bbc.co.uk/news/technology-68657840

Gerken, T. (2024b, November 28). Mark Zuckerberg dines with Donald Trump
at Mar-a-Lago. *BBC News.* https://www.bbc.co.uk/news/articles/c87x98
q8y08o

Giles, C., Goodman, J., & Robinson, O. (2021, January 11). Covid: The Truth
Behind Videos of "Empty" Hospitals. *BBC News.* https://www.bbc.co.uk/
news/55560714

Gillmor, D. (2004). *We, the Media.* O'Reilly Media.

Goffman, E. (2022). *The Presentation of Self in Everyday Life.* Penguin Books
Ltd.

Gold, M. (2023, December 5). Trump Says He Wouldn't Be a Dictator, 'Except
for Day 1'. *New York Times.* https://www.nytimes.com/2023/12/05/us/
politics/trump-fox-news-abuse-power.html

Goldberg, J. (2020, September 3). Trump: Americans Who Died in War Are
"Losers" and "Suckers". *The Atlantic.* https://www.theatlantic.com/pol
itics/archive/2020/09/trump-americans-who-died-at-war-are-losers-and-suc
kers/615997/

Goldmacher, S., Haberman, M., Swan, J.: (2024, November 7). How Trump
Won, and How Harris Lost. *New York Times.* https://www.nytimes.com/
2024/11/07/us/politics/trump-win-election-harris.html

Goldsmith, J., & Wu, T. (2006). *Who Controls the Internet?* Oxford University
Press.

Gorman, S., & Spalding, R. (2021, January 1). Wisconsin Pharmacist Arrested
on Charges of Sabotaging COVID Vaccine Doses. *Reuters.* https://www.reu
ters.com/article/us-health-coronavirus-usa-pharmacist-idUSKBN2961YF

Grayling, A. C. (2018). *Democracy and Its Crisis.* Oneworld.

Gramlich, J., & Passel, J. S. (2024, September 27). U.S. Immigrant Population in 2023 Saw Largest Increase in More Than 20 Years. *Pew Research Centre.* https://www.pewresearch.org/short-reads/2024/09/27/u-s-immigrant-population-in-2023-saw-largest-increase-in-more-than-20-years/#:~:text=The%20number%20of%20immigrants%20living,from%20the%20U.S.%20Census%20Bureau.

Graves, L., & Cherubini, F. (2016). The Rise of Fact-Checking Sites in Europe. *Reuters Institute for the Study of Journalism.* https://reutersinstitute.politics.ox.ac.uk/our-research/rise-fact-checking-sites-europe

Gregory, B. (2024, February 10). Zombies and Capitalism: George A. Romero's Anti-Capitalist critique, and His Democratic, Collaborative Film-Making. *Culture Matters.* https://www.culturematters.org.uk/zombies-and-capitalism-george-a-romero-s-anti-capitalist-critique-and-his-democratic-collaborative-film-making/

Grusin, R. (2004). Premediation. *Criticism, 46*(1), 17–39.

Guardian Staff. (2024, October 29). Jeff Bezos Defends Decision to End Washington Post Endorsements. *The Guardian.* https://www.theguardian.com/technology/2024/oct/28/jeff-bezos-washington-post-endorsements

Guilluy, C. (2019). *Twilight of the Elites.* Yale University Press.

Guynn, J. (2020, November 17). You're the Ultimate Editor. Twitter's Jack Dorsey and Facebook's Mark Zuckerberg Accused of Censoring Conservatives. *USA Today.* https://eu.usatoday.com/story/tech/2020/11/17/facebook-twitter-dorsey-zuckerberg-donald-trump-conservative-bias-antitrust/6317585002/

Haberman, M., & Goldmacher, S. (2023, March 7). Trump, Vowing 'Retribution,' Foretells a Second Term of Spite. *The New York Times.* https://www.nytimes.com/2023/03/07/us/politics/trump-2024-president.html

Habermas, J. (1989). *The Structural Transformation of the Public Sphere.* Polity Press.

Hagey, K. (2021, May 19). Peter Thiel, J.D. Vance Invest in Rumble Video Platform Popular on Political Right. *The Wall Street Journal.* https://www.wsj.com/articles/peter-thiel-j-d-vance-invest-in-rumble-video-platform-popular-on-political-right-11621447661

Hallin, D. C. (1994). *We Keep America on Top of the World: Television Journalism and the Public Sphere.* Routledge.

Hancock, S. (2021, June 4). Kate Shemirani: Nurse Who Claimed 5G Caused Covid Symptoms and Spread Vaccine Misinformation Struck Off. *The Independent.* https://www.independent.co.uk/news/uk/home-news/kate-shemirani-covid-nurse-struck-off-b1859159.html

Happer, C. (2024). *The Construction of Public Opinion in a Digital Age.* Manchester University Press.

Happer, C., Hoskins, A., & Merrin, W. (2019). Weaponizing Reality: An Intro-
    duction to Trump's War on the Media. In C. Happer, A. Hoskins, & W.
    Merrin (Eds.), *Trump's Media War* (pp. 3–22). Palgrave Macmillan.
Harvey, D. (2000). *The Condition of Post-Modernity*. Blackwell Publishers Ltd.
Hayek, F. (2001). *The Road to Serfdom*. Routledge.
Heller, A. (2009). *Ayn Rand and the World She Made*. Anchor Books.
Henley, J. (2021, March 3). Dutch Covid Test Centre Hit by Suspected
    Bomb Attack. *The Guardian*. https://www.theguardian.com/world/2021/
    mar/03/dutch-covid-test-centre-hit-by-suspected-bomb-attack
Hern, A. (2020, May 7). 5G Conspiracy Theories Fuel Attacks on Tele-
    coms Workers. *The Guardian*. https://www.theguardian.com/business/
    2020/may/07/5g-conspiracy-theories-attacks-telecoms-covid
Hernandes, R., Aratani, L., & Craft, W. (2024, December 7). Tech
    Poured $394.1m into US Election as Musk and Crypto Giving Boomed.
    *The Guardian*. https://www.theguardian.com/us-news/2024/dec/07/cam
    paign-spending-crypto-tech-influence
Hertsgaard, M. (2017, March 1). Creating a Fox News for the Left. *Columbia
    Journalism Review*. https://www.cjr.org/special_report/creating-a-fox-news-
    for-the-left.php
Hirschman, A. O. (1970). *Exit, Voice and Loyalty*. Harvard University Press.
Hochschild, A. R. (2017). *Strangers in Their Own Land: Anger and Mourning
    on the American Right*. The New Press.
Hoffman, B., & Ware, J. (2024). *God, Guns and Sedition. Far-Right Terrorism
    in America*. Columbia University Press.
Hoggart, R. (2009). *The Uses of Literacy*. Penguin.
Hoppe, H. H. (2017). *Democracy. The God That Failed*. Routledge.
Hoskins, A. (2014). AI and Memory. *Memory, Mind & Media, 3*, e18. https://
    doi.org/10.1017/mem.2024.16
Hoskins, A., & O'Loughlin, B. (2009). *Television and Terror: Conflicting Times
    and the Crisis of News Discourse*. Palgrave Macmillan.
Howarth, J. (2024, June 13). How Many People Own Smartphones? (2024–
    2029). *Exploding Topics*. https://explodingtopics.com/blog/smartphone-
    stats
Hubler, S. (2024, November 6). Harris Asked Voters to Protect Democracy.
    Here's Why It Didn't Land. *New York Times*. https://www.nytimes.com/
    2024/11/06/us/politics/harris-voters-democracy.html
Hunt, E. (2017, January 22). Trump's Inauguration Crowd: Sean Spicer's
    Claims Versus the Evidence. *The Guardian*. https://www.theguardian.com/
    us-news/2017/jan/22/trump-inauguration-crowd-sean-spicers-claims-ver
    sus-the-evidence

Hutzler, A. (2024, November 18). Trump Confirms Plan to Declare National Emergency, Use Military for Mass Deportations. *ABC News*. https://abc news.go.com/Politics/trump-confirms-plan-declare-national-emergency-mil itary-mass/story?id=115963448

ICIJ. (2024). The Panama Papers. *International Consortium of Investigative Journalists*. https://www.icij.org/investigations/panama-papers/

Isidore, C. (2024, November 20). How Much of Musk's Wealth Comes from Tax Dollars and Government Help? *CNN*. https://amp.cnn.com/cnn/2024/11/20/business/elon-musk-wealth-government-help

Ivanova, I. (2022, November 21). These Formerly Banned Twitter Accounts Have Been Reinstated Since Elon Musk Took Over. *Money Watch*. https://www.cbsnews.com/news/twitter-accounts-reinstated-elon-musk-donald-trump-kanye-ye-jordan-peterson-kathy-griffin-andrew-tate/

Jackson, J. (2017, January 12). BBC Sets Up Team to Debunk Fake News. *The Guardian*. https://www.theguardian.com/media/2017/jan/12/bbc-sets-up-team-to-debunk-fake-news

Jarvis, J. (2017, February 19). Trump & the Press: A Murder-Suicide Pact. *BuzzMachine*. http://buzzmachine.com/2017/02/19/trump-press-murder-suicide-pact/

Jarvis, J. (2024, October 29). Why Are Liberals Infuriated with the Media? *Columbia Journalism Review*. https://www.cjr.org/analysis/liberals-infuri ated-media-cancel-subscription-editorial-endorsement-times-washington-post-jarvis.php

Jenkins, H. (2006). *Convergence Culture*. New York University Press.

Judis, J. B. (2016). *The Populist Explosion*. Columbia Global Reports.

Kakutani, M. (2018). *The Death of Truth*. William Collins.

Katersky, A., Santucci, J., & Faulders, K. (2023, March 31). Trump Becomes 1st Current or Former President to be Indicted. *abcnews*. https://abcnews.go.com/US/trump-1st-current-former-president-indicted-sources/story?id=97860580

Keen, A. (2007). *The Cult of the Amateur*. Nicholas Brealey.

Kellner, D. (1989). *Jean Baudrillard. From Marxism to Postmodernism and Beyond*. Polity Press.

Kellner, D., & Best, S. (Eds.). (1991). *Postmodern Theory. Critical Interrogations*. Macmillan Press.

Kennedy, L. (2015). Photojournalism and Warfare in a Postphotographic Age. *Photography and Culture, 8*(2), 159–171. https://doi.org/10.1080/175 14517.2015.1076242

Kessler, G. (2024, November 6). What I've Learned from 9 Years of Fact-Checking Donald Trump. *The Washington Post*. https://www.washingto npost.com/politics/2024/11/06/what-ive-learned-9-years-fact-checking-donald-trump/

Kilander, G. (2024, August 27). Trump Slammed for Flashing Smile and Making 'Disgraceful' Thumbs Up at Soldiers' Graves. *The Independent*. https://www.independent.co.uk/news/world/americas/us-politics/donald-trump-grave-soldiers-arlington-b2602463.html

Klein, E. (2024, November 3). There's Something Very Different About Harris vs. Trump. *New York Times*. https://www.nytimes.com/2024/11/03/opinion/trump-harris-election-day.html

Klippenstein, K. (2024, December 10). Exclusive: Luigi's Manifesto. *Ken Klippenstein*. https://www.kenklippenstein.com/p/luigis-manifesto

Knibbs, K. (2024, October 28). AI Slop Is Flooding Medium. *Wired*. https://www.wired.com/story/ai-generated-medium-posts-content-moderation/

Koran, M. (2019, November 8). Anonymous Tell-All Book Likens Trump to '12-Year-Old in Air Traffic Control Tower'—Report. *The Guardian*. https://www.theguardian.com/us-news/2019/nov/07/anonymous-trump-administration-book

Kosseff, J. (2019). *The Twenty-Six Words That Created the Internet*. Cornell University Press.

Kristev, I., & Holmes, S. (2019). *The Light That Failed*. Allen Lane.

Kurzweil, R. (2005). *The Singularity is Near*. Gerald Duckworth and Co., Ltd.

Land, N. (2011). *Fanged Noumena. Collected Writings 1997–2007*. Urbanomic.

Land, N. (2023). *The Dark Enlightenment*. Imperium Press.

Lanier, J. (2011). *You Are Not a Gadget: A Manifesto*. Penguin.

Lawrence, A. (2024, April 21). Racist Dog Whistle: The Right Wing Has Weaponized "DEI", *The Guardian*. https://www.theguardian.com/culture/2024/apr/21/dei-language-conservatives-baltimore

Leadbetter, C. (2008). *We Think: The Power of Mass Creativity*. Profile Books.

Leonhardt, D. (2024, December 11). The Largest Immigration Surge in U.S. History. *New York Times*. https://www.nytimes.com/2024/12/11/briefing/the-largest-immigration-surge-in-us-history.html

Levin, B. (2020, February 11). Trump Claims Coronavirus Will "Miraculously" Go Away by April. *Vanity Fair*. https://www.vanityfair.com/news/2020/02/donald-trump-coronavirus-warm-weather?srsltid=AfmBOorjerjt35c7FT_i_ej-B2qy8psV7bfw1nfw58wGYSdDE-R1xsl5

Levitsky, S., & Ziblatt, D. (2018). *How Democracies Die*. Penguin.

Lindqvist, S. (1996). *Exterminate All the Brutes*. Granta Books.

Lippmann, W. (2007). *Public Opinion*. BN Publishing.

Lipstadt, D. (2005). *Denial. Holocaust History on Trial*. Harper Collins.

Locke, J. (1965). *Two Treatises of Government*. New York: Mentor Books, New American Library. https://press-pubs.uchicago.edu/founders/documents/v1ch4s1.html

Looker, R. (2024a, July 26). JD Vance Defends 'Childless Cat Ladies' Comment After Backlash. *BBC News*. https://www.bbc.co.uk/news/articles/c147yn4xxx4o

Looker, R. (2024b, July 31). "Is She Black or Indian?": Trump Questions Harris' Racial Identity. *BBC News*. https://www.bbc.co.uk/news/articles/c06k07dn1zjo

LSE. (2016, July 1). Journalistic Representations of Jeremy Corbyn in the British Press. *Media@LSEReport*. https://www.lse.ac.uk/media-and-communications/assets/documents/research/projects/corbyn/Cobyn-Report.pdf

Luce, E. (2017). *The Retreat of Western Liberalism*. Little Brown and Co.

Luscombe, R. (2024, September 15). Musk Says Humans Can Be on Mars in Four Years. Many Laugh, but Some See Purpose. *The Guardian*. https://www.theguardian.com/technology/2024/sep/15/musk-humans-live-on-mars-spacex

MacKinnon, R. (2012). *Consent of the Networked*. Basic Books.

Mansell, W. (2020, February 13). Man Pleads Guilty to Terrorism Charge After Blocking Hoover Dam Bridge with Armored Truck. *ABC News*. https://abcnews.go.com/US/man-pleads-guilty-terrorism-charge-blocking-bridge-armored/story?id=68955385

Mansfield, E. (2024, July 17). Peter Thiel and JD Vance: How PayPal founder boosted VP Candidate's Political Career. *US Today News*. https://eu.usatoday.com/story/news/politics/elections/2024/07/17/peter-thiel-boosted-jd-vance-career/74397520007/

Marcuse, H. (1991). *One Dimensional Man*. Routledge.

Margaret Thatcher Foundation. (1987, September 23). 1987 Sep 23 Margaret Thatcher Interview for Woman's Own ("No Such Thing [as Society]"). *Margaret Thatcher Foundation*. https://www.margaretthatcher.org/document/106689

Martin, J., Haberman, M., & Burns, A. (2016, October 8). Lewd Donald Trump Tape Is a Breaking Point for Many in the G.O.P. *The New York Times*. https://www.nytimes.com/2016/10/09/us/politics/donald-trump-campaign.html

Marwick, A., & Lewis, R. (2017, May 15). Media Manipulation and Disinformation Online. Data & Society Research Institute Report. https://datasociety.net/pubs/oh/DataAndSociety_MediaManipulationAndDisinformationOnline.pdf

Marx, K., & Engels, F. (2004). *Manifesto of the Communist Party*. https://www.marxists.org/archive/marx/works/download/pdf/Manifesto.pdf

Mashable. (2016). Insult After Insult. *Mashable*. https://mashable.com/feature/trump-timeline

Mauss, M. (1990). *The Gift. The Form and Reasons for Exchange in Archaic Societies*. Routledge.

Massie, G. (2021, November 12). Jeff Bezos Predicts People Will One Day Be Born in Space and "Visit Earth the Way You Visit Yellowstone National Park". *The Independent*. https://www.independent.co.uk/space/bezos-space-colonies-earth-tourism-b1956834.html

McCarthy, B. (2024, August 12). Trump Baselessly Accuses Harris of Faking Crowd Size with AI. *AFP Fact Check*. https://factcheck.afp.com/doc.afp.com.36E79DM

McCarthy, J. (2007). What Is Artificial Intelligence? https://www-formal.stanford.edu/jmc/whatisai.pdf

McCarthy, T. (2020, April 14). "It Will Disappear": The Disinformation Trump Spread about the Coronavirus—Timeline. *The Guardian*. https://www.theguardian.com/us-news/2020/apr/14/trump-coronavirus-alerts-disinformation-timeline

McCarthy, T., & Belam, M. (2020, December 10). US Records More Than 3,000 Covid Deaths a day for the First Time. *The Guardian*. https://www.theguardian.com/world/2020/dec/10/us-3000-covid-deaths-coronavirus-day-first-time

McIntyre, L. (2018). *Post-Truth*. MIT Press.

McLuhan, M. (1994). *Understanding Media: The Extensions of Man*. MIT Press.

McLuhan, M., & Fiore, Q. (1996). *The Medium Is the Massage*. Hardwired.

McMahon, L. (2024, December 12). Mark Zuckerberg's Meta Donates $1m to Trump Fund. *BBC News*. https://www.bbc.co.uk/news/articles/c8j9e1x9z2xo

McQuarrie, M. (2016, September 29). From Solidarity to Trump: White Working Class Culture in the Rust Belt. *Hampton*. https://www.hamptonthink.org/read/from-solidarity-to-trump-white-working-class-culture-in-the-rust-belt

Meko, H. (2024, December 7). Some on Social Media See Suspect in C.E.O. Killing as a Folk Hero. *New York Times*. https://www.nytimes.com/2024/12/07/nyregion/unitedhealthcare-ceo-shooting-suspect.html

Merrin, W. (2005). Skylights Onto Infinity: The World in a Stereoscope. In S. Popple & V. Toulmin (Eds.), *Visual Delights II* (pp. 161–174). John Libby Press.

Merrin, W. (2014). *Media Studies* 2.0. Abingdon, Oxon: Routledge.

Merrin, W. (2018). *Digital War*. Routledge.

Merrin, W. (2021). From Television to the Internet: From the Reality of Terror to Reality Terrorism. *Critical Studies on Terrorism, 14*(4), 450–454. https://www.tandfonline.com/doi/full/10.1080/17539153.2021.1982461

Merrin, W., & Hoskins, A. (2020). Tweet Fast and Kill Things: Digital War. *Digital War, 1*, 184–193. https://doi.org/10.1057/s42984-020-00002-1

Merrin, W., & Hoskins, A. (2024). Sharded War: Seeing, Not Sharing. *Digital War, 5*(1), 115–118. https://doi.org/10.1057/s42984-023-00086-5

Metz, C. (2024, December 13). OpenAI's Sam Altman to Donate $1 Million to Trump's Inaugural Fund. *New York Times*. https://www.nytimes.com/2024/12/13/technology/openai-sam-altman-trump-inauguration.html

Michael, G. (2022, July 27). An Antidemocratic Philosophy Called 'Neoreaction' Is Creeping into GOP Politics. *The Conversation*. https://theconversation.com/an-antidemocratic-philosophy-called-neoreaction-is-creeping-into-gop-politics-182581

Michallon, C. (2019, October 29). Trump's Baghdadi Address Compared to Obama's Bin Laden Speech in Hilarious Mash-Up. *The Independent*. https://www.independent.co.uk/arts-entertainment/tv/news/trump-obama-kimmel-video-baghdadi-obama-osama-bin-laden-speech-a9176331.html

Mind. (2024, November 13). Mind Cymru Urges Welsh Government to Take Action on Addressing the Root Causes of Poor Mental Health in Wales. *Mind*. https://www.mind.org.uk/news-campaigns/news/mind-cymru-urges-welsh-government-to-take-action-on-addressing-the-root-causes-of-poor-mental-health-in-wales/

Mishra, P. (2017). *Age of Anger: A History of the Present*. Allen Lane.

Mistry, P. (2024, August 16). "Keyboard Warrior" Jailed for Part in UK Disorder. *BBC News*. https://www.bbc.co.uk/news/articles/c5y3gre3y9yo

Moravec, H. (1988). *Mind Children*. Harvard University Press.

Morozov, E. (2011). *The Net Delusion*. Allen Lane.

Morgan, E. S. (1989). *Inventing the People. The Rise of Popular Sovereignty in England and America*. W. W. Norton.

Mounk, Y. (2018). *The People Vs. Democracy*. Harvard University Press.

Mudde, C. (2017). *Populism: A Very Short Introduction*. Oxford University Press.

Müller, J. W. (2017). *What Is Populism?* Penguin.

Müller, J. W. (2024, November 9). Why Has the American Center Right Disappeared from the Ballot Box? *The Guardian*. https://www.theguardian.com/commentisfree/2024/nov/09/republican-center-right

National Archive. (2024, August 27). Declaration of Independence: A Transcription. *National Archives*. https://www.archives.gov/founding-docs/declaration-transcript

Nelson, L. (2018, January 5). Internet Falls for Trump-"Gorilla Channel" Parody. *Politico*. https://www.politico.com/story/2018/01/05/trump-gorilla-channel-parody-326374

Norris, C. (1990). *What's Wrong with Postmodernism*. Harvester Wheatsheaf.

Norris, C. (1992). *Uncritical Theory. Postmodernism, Intellectuals, and the Gulf War*. Lawrence and Wishart.

Noys, B. (2014). *Malign Velocities. Accelerationism and Capitalism*. Zero Books.

Nyhan, B., & Reifler, J. (2010). When Corrections Fail: The Persistence of Political Misperceptions. *Polit Behavior, 32*, 303–330. https://doi.org/10.1007/s11109-010-9112-2

Oates, S. (2024). Trump's Imagined Reality Is America's New Reality. https://www.electionanalysis.ws/us/president2024/section-1-democracy-at-stake/trumps-imagined-reality-is-americas-new-reality/

O'Neil, J. (2021, February 8). Iranian Cleric Claims COVID-19 Vaccine Turns People into "Homosexuals". *New York Post*. https://nypost.com/2021/02/08/iranian-cleric-says-covid-vax-turns-people-into-homosexuals/

Online Etymology Dictionary. (2022). Public (adj). https://www.etymonline.com/word/public

O'Reilly, T. (2005, September 30). What Is Web 2.0? *O'Reilly*. https://www.oreilly.com/pub/a/web2/archive/what-is-web-20.html

Owens, L. (2024, December 20). Elon Musk Wants to Pay for His Tax Cuts With Your Social Security and Medicare. *Rolling Stone*. https://www.rollingstone.com/politics/political-commentary/elon-musk-vivek-trump-tax-cuts-social-security-medicare-1235212608/

Paine, T. (1985). *Rights of Man*. Penguin.

Pariser, E. (2011). *The Filter Bubble*. Viking Books.

Parveen, N., & Waterson, J. (2020, April 4). UK Phone Masts Attacked Amid 5G-Coronavirus Conspiracy Theory. *The Guardian*. https://www.theguardian.com/uk-news/2020/apr/04/uk-phone-masts-attacked-amid-5g-coronavirus-conspiracy-theory

PBS. (2017, January 18). When It Comes to Inaugural Crowds, Does Size Matter? *PBS News*. https://www.pbs.org/newshour/nation/comes-inaugural-crowds-size-matter

Peat, J. (2024, December 11). Elon Musk: "Homelessness Is a Lie". *The London Economic*. https://www.thelondoneconomic.com/news/elon-musk-homelessness-is-a-lie-387078/

Pengelly, M. (2023, December 27). Top Trumps: The 10 Worst Things the Former President Said This Year. *The Guardian*. https://www.theguardian.com/us-news/2023/dec/27/worst-things-that-trump-has-said

Pengelly, M. (2024, November 8). Nancy Pelosi Says Biden's Delay in Exiting Race Blew Democrats' Chances. *The Guardian*. https://www.theguardian.com/us-news/2024/nov/08/nancy-pelosi-biden-democrats-election-loss

Petri, A. I. (2023, April 22). Book Bans Are on the Rise in U.S. Schools, Fuelled by New Laws in Republican-led States. *Los Angeles Times*. https://www.latimes.com/world-nation/story/2023-04-22/book-bans-soaring-schools-new-laws-republican-states

Picchi, A. (2024, December 17). 50 Years of Tax Cuts for the Rich Failed to Trickle Down, Economics Study Says. *CBS News*. https://www.cbsnews.com/news/tax-cuts-rich-50-years-no-trickle-down/

Pietsch, B. (2020, July 12). Texas Hospital Says Man, 30, Died After Attending a "Covid Party". *New York Times*. https://www.nytimes.com/2020/07/12/us/30-year-old-covid-party-death.html

Plato. (1988). *The Republic*. London: Penguin Classics.

Politico. (2024, November 6). Tracking the Trump Criminal Cases. *Politico.* https://www.politico.com/interactives/2023/trump-criminal-invest igations-cases-tracker-list/

Postman, N. (1987). *Amusing Ourselves to Death: Public Discourse in the Age of Show Business*. Methuen.

Quinn, B. (2021, February 4). Piers Corbyn Arrested Over Leaflets Comparing Vaccine Programme to Auschwitz. *The Guardian*. https://www.theguardian. com/uk-news/2021/feb/04/piers-corbyn-arrested-over-leaflets-comparing-covid-vaccine-programme-to-auschwitz

Rand, A. (1964). *The Virtue of Selfishness*. Penguin.

Rand, A. (2007a). *The Fountainhead*. Penguin.

Rand, A. (2007b). *Atlas Shrugged*. Penguin.

Ray, R., & Gibbons, A. (2021). Why Are States Banning Critical Race Theory? *Brookings*, November, Musk's support for the populist right would culminate domestically in his financial and political support for Donald Trump in November 2024. Trump's victory speech acknowledged the role of Musk, calling him 'a super genius' (Ray 2024)

Ray, S. (2021, July 15). Trump Kompromat Claimed: Kremlin Documents Reportedly Show Putin Conspiring For Billionaire. *Forbes*. https://www.for bes.com/sites/siladityaray/2021/07/15/trump-kompromat-claimed-report-says-kremlin-documents-show-putin-conspiring-for-billionaire/

Ray, S. (2024, November 6). Trump Hails "Super Genius" Elon Musk in Victory Speech—Ahead of Likely Election Win. *Forbes*. https://www.forbes. com/sites/siladityaray/2024/11/06/trump-hails-super-genius-elon-musk-in-victory-speech-ahead-of-likely-election-win/

Reilly, R. J. (2024, November 3). Days Before the Election, DOJ Continues to Prosecute New Jan. 6 Cases. *NBC News*. https://www.nbcnews.com/pol itics/justice-department/new-jan-6-arrests-sentences-ahead-2024-election-rcna178505

Raymond, E. (1998). The Cathedral and the Bazaar. *First Monday*. https://fir stmonday.org/ojs/index.php/fm/article/download/578/499?inline=1

Rheingold, H. (1993). *The Virtual Community*. https://www.rheingold.com/vc/book/intro.html

Rose-Stockwell, T. (2023). *Outrage Machine*. Piatkus.

Rothschild, M. (2021). *The Storm Is Upon Us. How QAnon Became a Movement, A Cult and Conspiracy Theory About Everything*. Monoray.

Roush, T. (2023, December 12). Donald Trump Releases 'Mugshot Edition' Digital Trading Cards—Offers Pieces of Suit from Fulton County Arrest. *Forbes*. https://www.forbes.com/sites/tylerroush/2023/12/12/donald-trump-releases-mugshot-edition-digital-trading-cards-offers-pieces-of-suit-from-fulton-county-arrest/

Runciman, D. (2018). *How Democracy Ends*. Profile Books.

Sainato, M. (2024, October 27). Bezos Faces Criticism After Executives Met with Trump on Day of Post's Non-Endorsement. *The Guardian*. https://www.theguardian.com/media/2024/oct/27/bezos-washington-post-non-endorsement-election

Sandford, D., Sherlock, G., & Mullen, T. (2024, August 1). Teen, 17, Accused of Southport Murders Named. *BBC News*. https://www.bbc.co.uk/news/articles/c6p2yrg3pvpo

Savage, C. (2021, January 10). Incitement to Riot? What Trump Told Supporters Before Mob Stormed Capitol. *New York Times*. https://www.nytimes.com/2021/01/10/us/trump-speech-riot.html

Schaake, M. (2024). *The Tech Coup*. Princeton University Press.

Schleifer, T., & Yaffe-Bellany, D. (2024, December 14). In Display of Fealty, Tech Industry Curries Favor With Trump. *New York Times*. https://www.nytimes.com/2024/12/14/technology/trump-tech-amazon-meta-openai.html

Schwab, K., & Malleret, T. (2020). *Covid-19: The Great Reset*, Cologny/Geneva: World Economic Forum.

Shirky, C. (2008). *Here Comes Everybody*. Allen Lane.

Silverman, C. (2016, December 15). Facebook Is Turning to Fact-Checkers to Fight Fake News. *BuzzFeedNews*. https://www.buzzfeed.com/craigsilverman/facebook-and-fact-checkers-fight-fake-news?bftwnews&utm_term=.swejxd4W2#.fddVMPQr7

Silverstone, R. (2002). Mediating Catastrophe: September 11 and the Crisis of the Other. https://www.infoamerica.org/documentos_pdf/silverstone07.pdf

Sky News. (2019, August 20). Facebook 'Suppresses' Conservative Views, Says Report. *Sky News*. https://news.sky.com/story/facebook-suppresses-conservative-views-says-report-11789975

Slobodian, Q. (2018). *Globalists*. Harvard University Press.

Sloterdijk, P. (2016). *Foam: Spheres Vol. III*. Semiotext(e).

Smith, D. (2020a, March 21). Trump Throws Tantrum over Coronavirus Question: "You're a Terrible Reporter". *The Guardian*. https://www.theguardian.com/us-news/2020/mar/20/trump-coronavirus-question-attack-reporter-over-fears

Smith, D. (2020b, November 4). 'Authoritarian': Trump Condemned for Falsely Claiming Election Victory. *The Guardian*. https://www.theguardian.com/us-news/2020/nov/04/donald-trump-election-joe-biden-vote-count

Smith, D. (2023, October 25). Nearly One in Four Americans Believe Political Violence Justified to 'Save' US. *The Guardian*. https://www.theguardian.com/us-news/2023/oct/25/us-political-violence-justified-survey

Smith, H., & Burrows, R. (2021). Software, Sovereignty and the Post-Neoliberal Politics of Exit. *Theory, Culture and Society, 38*(6). https://journals.sagepub.com/doi/10.1177/0263276421999439

Sommer, W. (2023). *Trust the Plan: The Rise of QAnon and the Conspiracy That Reshaped the World*. Fourth Estate.

Sontag, S. (2003). *Regarding the Pain of Others*. Farrar, Straus and Giroux.

Spring, M. (2024, August 7). What is Elon Musk's Game Plan? *BBC Indepth*. https://www.bbc.co.uk/news/articles/cze5gd1jzkeo

Srinivasan, B. (2013). Silicon Valley's Ultimate Exit. https://genius.com/Balaji-srinivasan-silicon-valleys-ultimate-exit-annotated

Srinivasan, B. (2022). *The Network State: How To Start a New Country*. PDF: https://thenetworkstate.com/book/tns.pdf

Srnicek, N., & Williams, A. (2013). *#Accelerate Manifesto: For an Accelerationist Politics*. https://criticallegalthinking.com/2013/05/14/accelerate-manifesto-for-an-accelerationist-politics/

Srnicek, N., & Williams, A. (2015). *Inventing the Future*. Verso.

Standing, G. (2016). *The Precariat*. Bloomsbury.

Statista. (2024). Long-Term Migration Figures in the United Kingdom from 1964 to 2024. *Statista*. https://www.statista.com/statistics/283287/net-migration-figures-of-the-united-kingdom-y-on-y/

Stedman Jones, D. (2012). *Masters of the Universe*. Princeton University Press.

Steger, M. (2017). *Globalization. A Very Short Introduction*. Oxford University Press.

Stencel, M., Ryan, E., & Luther, J. (2024, May 30). With Half the Planet Going to the Polls in 2024, Fact-Checking Sputters. *Reporters' Lab*. https://reporterslab.org/with-half-the-planet-going-to-the-polls-in-2024-fact-checking-sputters/

Stracqualursi, V. (2024, October 14). Trump Suggests Using Military Against 'Enemy from Within' on Election Day. *CNN*. https://edition.cnn.com/2024/10/13/politics/trump-military-enemy-from-within-election-day/index.html

Streeck, W. (2024). *Taking Back Control States and State Systems After Globalism*. Verso.

Streitfeld, D. (2016, October 15). Peter Thiel to Donate $1.25 Million in Support of Donald Trump. *New York Times*. https://www.nytimes.com/2016/10/16/technology/peter-thiel-donald-j-trump.html

Tait, R. (2024, July 25). Trump Monetizes Assassination Attempt by Using Photo as Book Cover. *The Guardian*. https://www.theguardian.com/us-news/article/2024/jul/25/trump-shooting-photo-book-cover

TheLotrTV. (2013, August 12). The Lord of the Rings—The Mirror of Galadriel (Extended Edition HD). *Youtube*. https://www.youtube.com/watch?v=K3VOf3CBGvw

Thiel, P. (2009, April 13). The Education of a Libertarian. *Cato Unbound*. https://www.cato-unbound.org/2009/04/13/peter-thiel/education-libertarian/

Thomas, D., & Fleury, M. (2024, August 6). Elon Musk sues Unilever and Mars over X "boycott". *BBC News*. https://www.bbc.co.uk/news/articles/cn4779 8gxx4o

Thompson, S. A. (2024, December 13). I Traded My News Apps for Rumble, the Right-Wing YouTube. Here's What I Saw. *New York Times*. https://www.nytimes.com/interactive/2024/12/13/business/rumble-trump-bongino-kirk.html

TOI Tech Deck. (2024, June 17). Elon Musk's X Banned over 2 Lakh Accounts in India in May. *Times of India*. https://timesofindia.indiatimes.com/technology/tech-news/elon-musks-x-banned-over-2-lakh-accounts-in-india-in-may/articleshow/111058079.cms

Tufekci, Z. (2024, December 6). The Rage and Glee That Followed a C.E.O.'s Killing Should Ring All Alarms. *New York Times*. https://www.nytimes.com/2024/12/06/opinion/united-health-care-ceo-shooting.html

Turkle, S. (1996). *Life on the Screen*. Weidenfeld and Nicolson.

Turkle, S. (2011). *Alone Together*. Basic Books.

Turness, D. (2023, May 22). Explaining the 'How'—The Launch of BBC Verify. *BBC News*. https://www.bbc.co.uk/news/uk-65650822

United States Attorney Office. (2022, April 13). Former San Pedro Train Engineer Sentenced to 3 Years in Prison for Intentionally Derailing Locomotive Near U.S. Navy Hospital Ship. *United States Attorney's Office. Central District of California*. https://www.justice.gov/usao-cdca/pr/former-san-pedro-train-engineer-sentenced-3-years-prison-intentionally-derailing

USA Facts. (2024). How Many People Are Coming to the US and Where Are They Coming From? *USA Facts*. https://usafacts.org/state-of-the-union/immigration/

Vaidhyanathan, S. (2024, November 20). Elon Musk Is the Ultimate Chaos Agent. *The Guardian*. https://www.theguardian.com/commentisfree/2024/dec/20/elon-musk-chaos-agent

Vance, J. D. (2017). *Hillbilly Elegy*. Harper Collins.

Volpe, J. D. (2024, November 11). Democrats Could Have Won. Our Excuses Mask a Devastating Reality. *New York Times*. https://www.nytimes.com/2024/11/11/opinion/kamala-harris-young-voters.html

Walker, A. R. (2024, November 8). Black People Across US Receive Racist Text Messages After Trump's Win. *The Guardian*. https://www.theguardian.com/us-news/2024/nov/08/racist-text-messages-trump-win

Waterson, J. (2017, March 15). Russia Today Says It Wants to Help Facebook Combat Fake News. *BuzzFeedNews*. https://www.buzzfeed.com/jimwaterson/russia-today-says-it-wants-to-help-facebook-combat-fake-news?utm_term=.joZL1AaX3#.vcjae5Dwk

Warzel, C. (2024a, November 8). Bad News: Legacy Media Must Compete Against a Choose-Your-Own-Adventure Reality. *The Atlantic.* https://www. theatlantic.com/technology/archive/2024/11/you-are-the-media-now/680 602/

Warzel, C. (2024b, August 21). The MAGA Aesthetic Is AI Slop. *The Atlantic.* https://www.theatlantic.com/technology/archive/2024/08/ trump-posts-ai-image/679540/

The Washington Post (2021) Fact Checker database as at 20th January. https:// www.washingtonpost.com/graphics/politics/trump-claims-database/?itid=lk_ inline_manual_15

Weise, K., & Haberman, M. (2024, December 12). Amazon Plans $1 Million Donation to Trump's Inaugural Fund. *New York Times.* https://www.nyt imes.com/2024/12/12/technology/amazon-trump-inauguration.html

White, N. (2024, August 7). Far Right Thugs Stop Cars to Check If Drivers Are White Before Letting Them Pass. *The Independent.* https://www.indepe ndent.co.uk/news/uk/home-news/far-right-race-riot-uk-b2591803.html

Wilson, J. (2019, August 1). Conspiracy Theories Like QAnon Could Fuel "Extremist" Violence, FBI Says. *The Guardian.* https://www.theguardian. com/us-news/2019/aug/01/conspiracy-theories-fbi-qanon-extremism

Wilson, J. (2024, December 21). He's Anti-democracy and Pro-Trump: The Obscure 'Dark Enlightenment' Blogger Influencing the next US Adminis-tration. *The Guardian.* https://www.theguardian.com/us-news/2024/dec/ 21/curtis-yarvin-trump

Wolf, M. (2018). *Fire and Fury.* Little, Brown Book Group.

Wollstonecraft, M. (2004). *A Vindication of the Rights of Women.* Penguin.

Woodward, A. (2021, June 24). OAN Host Suggests 'Traitors' Who 'Stole' Election Should Be Executed. *The Independent.* https://www.independent. co.uk/news/world/americas/us-politics/oan-executions-conspiracy-theory-qanon-b1872104.html

Woodward, A. (2024, December 13). Elon Musk Calls Homelessness a "Lie" and "Propaganda"—And Trump Is Listening. *The Independent.* https:// www.independent.co.uk/news/world/americas/us-politics/elon-musk-hom eless-trump-vivek-ramaswamy-b2663740.html

Wright, K., Scott, M., & Bunce, M. (2024). *Capturing News, Capturing Democracy: Trump and the Voice of America.* Oxford University Press.

Yarvin, C. (2022, March 31). The Cathedral or the Bizarre: America's Exper-iments with Democracy and Oligarchy Have Both Failed, Leaving Only One Option. *Tablet Magazine.* https://www.tabletmag.com/sections/news/ articles/the-cathedral-or-the-bizarre

Young, G. K. (2021). How Much Is Too Much: The Difficulties of Social Media Content Moderation. *Information & Communications Technology Law, 31*(1), 1–16. https://doi.org/10.1080/13600834.2021.1905593

Yousif, N. (2023, September 17). How the Fentanyl Crisis' Fourth Wave Has Hit Every Corner of the US. *BBC News*. https://www.bbc.co.uk/news/world-us-canada-66826895

Zarrell, R. (2014, July 20). Teen's Smiling Selfie at Auschwitz Goes Viral After Inciting Twitter Anger. *Buzzfeed News*. https://www.buzzfeednews.com/article/rachelzarrell/teens-smiling-selfie-at-auschwitz-goes-viral-after-inciting

Ziady, H. (2024, August 7). Elon Musk Says 'Civil War Is Inevitable' as UK Rocked by Far-Right Riots. He's Part of the Problem. *CNN*. https://edition.cnn.com/2024/08/06/tech/elon-musk-civil-war-uk-riots/index.html

Zimmer, B. (2010). On Language: Truthiness. *The New York Times Magazine*. https://www.nytimes.com/2010/10/17/magazine/17FOB-onlanguage-t.html

Zittrain, J. (2008). *The Future of the Net*. Penguin.

# INDEX

The manufacturer's authorised representative in the EU is Springer
Nature Customer Service Centre GmbH, Europaplatz 3, 69115 Heidelberg,
Germany. If you have any concerns regarding our products, please
contact ProductSafety@springernature.com

Printed and bound by CPI Group (UK) Ltd, Croydon, CR0 4YY
27/04/2026
02097563-0018